# SPIRITUAL
# REVOLUTION

# SPIRITUAL REVOLUTION

Experience the Supernatural in
Your Life Through Angelic Visitations,
Prophetic Dreams, and Miracles

PATRICIA KING

**Destiny Image® Publishers, Inc.**
**P.O. Box 310**
**Shippensburg, PA 17257-0310**

*"Speaking to the Purposes of God for this Generation*
*and for the Generations to Come."*

For Worldwide Distribution, Printed in the U.S.A.

ISBN 10: 0-7684-2356-2
ISBN 13: 978-0-7684-2356-3

This book and all other Destiny Image, Revival Press, MercyPlace, Fresh Bread, Destiny Image Fiction, and Treasure House books are available at Christian bookstores and distributors worldwide.

For a U.S. bookstore nearest you, call
**1-800-722-6774.**

For more information on foreign distributors, call
**717-532-3040.**

Or reach us on the Internet:
**www.destinyimage.com**

1 2 3 4 5 6 7 8 9 10 11 / 09 08 07 06

# DEDICATION

To every dissatisfied and hungry believer who longs for more!

# Acknowledgements

### My Husband and Team

Who have been true friends.

### James W. Goll

Who has been there to confront, support, and encourage me throughout this project.

### Wesley and Stacey Campbell

Who pastored me in the midst of crisis.

### Don Milam

Who has been patient and supportive.

### Grace Growers

Who have sharpened me as iron sharpens iron.

# ENDORSEMENTS

Patricia King is a modern day missionary reaching out to a hurting world with the redemptive message of God's great love. You will be greatly encouraged by the impact of her book. This book will cause you to draw ever closer to the Father and the biblical revelations will aid you to better understand these current days. It is a joy to recommend not only the book but also the author—you will be blessed by both.

Bobby Conner
Eagles View Ministries
www.bobbyconner.org

Patricia King's passion for the Lord is genuine and contagious. She carries a forerunner anointing that is blazing a trail that paves the way for the end-time ministry to flourish. Her book *Spiritual Revolution* is another powerful tool from the arsenal of weapons that the Lord has entrusted to her to equip His people. Not only will this timely book provide strategic insight and sound biblical teaching, but also inspiration to mobilize God's army into its divine destiny. The prophet David asked, "is there not a cause." This book answers that question with profound clarity. The Lord Jesus is about to revolutionize our present understanding of His Kingdom and His Presence in the earth.

Paul Keith Davis
Founder, White Dove Ministries
Orange Beach, Alabama

This book is why I am a publisher! God called me to publish the prophets. There are men and women who have the courage to see what has not been seen and then write it down so those who read it may run. *Spiritual Revolution* is one of those books that will challenge you to reach beyond the ordinary and grasp the extraordinary reality of living and experiencing the supernatural lifestyle Jesus intends for us to have. Patricia King is a forerunner, a pioneer in the prophetic. Like all pioneers she is plowing the ground for others and making discoveries that will bless the whole Body of Christ. I am proud to publish this book and I champion her cause as a prophetic pioneer.

Don Nori
CEO and Founder
Destiny Image Publishers

Wow! What a book! Patricia King has once again taken great risk to go beyond the theories of Christianity, into the actual pursuit of experiencing God in biblical proportions. And she has done so with love and scholarship. Because of her heart to equip the saints, this book gives us the hope of her amazing insights and supernatural experiences becoming normal in God's people again. Until then we must honor and follow the "Patricia Kings" in this world who labor to bring us the *more* of the gospel. Thank you Patricia!

Bill Johnson
Author and international ministry speaker

There are many who write books on a subject they love or know well, but there are others who write a book because it is a life message. That is the case with this new book. For Patricia, experiencing the wonders of the heavenly realm is something she lives on a daily basis and she is passionate about sharing this joy with others. Let this book teach, inspire, and lead you to new depths of heavenly wonder.

Dick Dewert, B.Th., D.D.
President, Founder, The Miracle Channel
Alberta, Canada
www.miraclechannel.ca

Patricia King's *Spiritual Revolution* fills a gap that few writers can fill. She causes, through her anointed writing, a spiritual hunger and thirst for the supernatural that all Christians simply must have in order to move to the next level in Christ. Jesus was and is a supernatural Lord, and while He made us to walk on a "natural" earth, we must not forget—in fact we need to be reminded constantly—that a supernatural God made this earth and He invades His own creation on a daily basis with supernatural activity. It's for God to intervene—it's for us to discern His intervention. *Spiritual Revolution* caused me to want more—and then yet more beyond that—of the supernatural workings of God. But don't take my word for it and don't take Patricia King's word for it. Take the Scripture's word for it that she so poignantly weaves throughout the book.

Steve Shultz
Founder, THE ELIJAH LIST
Albany, Oregon
www.elijahlist.com

# TABLE OF CONTENTS

# Foreword

## BY JAMES W. GOLL

Pioneers pave the way! Pioneers pay a cost! Pioneers do not stop at the last move of God and say, "That's far enough. That is all there is!" These forerunners go before the main stream carving a course on a seemingly uncharted map so that others can cross on over into the truths, understandings, and experiences that these breakers have already entered into.

That is what this book, *Spiritual Revolution*, is all about! Patricia King, as a true forerunner has said in her heart, "The Holy Spirit is real! Heaven is real! The prophetic is real! Let's hear what God is declaring in this hour and move forward together in Christ Jesus!" Yes, a quick and sudden change of expression of Christianity is upon us. Yes, there's going to be a revolution—a spiritual one, in fact!

Do you want to learn how to bring Heaven down to earth and help other believers learn of their authority and position seated with Christ Jesus in the heavenly places? Want to be so heavenly minded that you will be of earthly good? Want to experience

Jacob's ladder coming down and the angels ascending and descending? Do you want to see open heavens over your life, family, neighborhood, and city? Patricia King believes that this *Seer* dimension is not just available for a few anointed prophets—she believes that you too can experience this "More Realm of God" for yourself!

Want to have your heart tuned into what Heaven is saying? Then keep reading! Glimpses of another realm will be granted to you from Scripture, testimony and yes, experience! In fact, you are already seated with Christ far above all the powers of this temporary present darkness. Want to learn more? Then blaze a trail with Patricia King and other pioneers who have signed up for something Extreme in the Prophetic in their lives.

Don't just read another enlightening book—experience the book—become the book! Go on an adventure—live the life—devour *Spiritual Revolution*! As we say in our ministry, "Experience His Presence and Release His Power!"

With prayer and great expectation, I commend to you the life and ministry of Patricia King. Let *Spiritual Revolution* march forth!

James W. Goll
Encounters Network
Author of *The Seer, Dream Language,*
*The Lost Art of Practicing His Presence, God Encounters.*

# A REVOLUTION?

Revolution: *A sudden or momentous change in a situation.*

*A sudden or momentous change*—this is, without a doubt, a very accurate description of what is taking place today in the 21st-century church. Everything is changing quickly. If the church environment has not changed yet in your circles, it will; and the church ten years from now will look completely different from what we see currently.

What is the church going to look like in the midst of revolution? No one can give a full answer to that right now, but one thing we can discern for sure—the cloud is moving and we had best move with it. Just as the Lord led Israel through the wilderness by a pillar of cloud by day and a pillar of fire by night, He is also leading us. Although we will not be able to fully figure out all that He is doing in this time of revolution, we need to follow His Spirit's leading, remain immersed in the Word, and trust Him to bring us into the land of promise.

We must be willing to lay everything on the altar, including our opinions, our programs, and our old structures. We must be willing to follow Him with passion and devotion as the revolution unfolds. This emerging revolution will manifest God's goodness, power, glory, supernatural signs, wonders, and miracles. The revolution will transition a powerless church into a light-radiating Body of His presence, full of pulsating heavenly presence and power. The revolution will call us to walk like Jesus did in the Gospels and as the apostles did in the Book of Acts. The revolution will call for a people clothed with heavenly power and godly character. What a day we are living in!

Are you ready for it? Perhaps some of what the Lord is about to do will shock and awe many people. As in past historical moves of revolution, there will be those who resist and harden their heart, desiring to hold on to old ways and mind-sets. Change is often difficult because it forces us to rethink hardened opinions and be willing to remove ourselves from the rut of our comfortable lifestyles. However, in spite of those who resist the revolution, there will be those who embrace it, jumping on board and following Jesus into new and uncharted territory. Some things that God will manifest in these coming days have never been done before, things that will stretch our imagination and challenge our intellect.

Revolutions are usually *messy* to some degree. It takes time for individuals to understand change and new ways. Revolution produces conflict, and conflict with its pressures will test and confirm what is true and real. Revolution ignites fires—fires of passion and fires of purging. During the coming days, it will be important for all to draw close to Jesus, to His counsel and wisdom. It will be important not to *react* to what we see but to *respond* to the Spirit as we go to Him and ask for insight.

The ways of God stretch beyond our ability to imagine what He will do. And when we are stretched beyond our comfort zones, we can easily become afraid of the new emerging spiritual environment and be tempted to limit ourselves to what we have learned and experienced in the past. During times of revolution, we must keep our hearts open and at the same time remain steadfast within the framework and guidelines of the Holy Scriptures. We must always uphold God's character and nature.

Every new birth requires diligence not only in the breaking of the membrane, which the prophetic and apostolic often accomplish, but also in the nurturing and maturation process that the pastoral and teaching ministries provide. The evangelists also need to be on board in order to proclaim the good news of the fresh move and ignite the Body with passion for this new season.

In the coming spiritual revolution, a spiritual hunger will surface like never before. You will see hunger for the supernatural and for the raw power of God. Young people especially will search for deeper meaning to life. They are not looking for a church service to attend or for a club to join. They are searching for spiritual realities that transcend religious traditions. They are looking for models that can be applied to their lives. They are looking for what is truly real and for what is eternal. They are weary of simply hearing the words preached. They want demonstration. Paul understood this principle, and we too must recapture the apostolic pattern.

*And my message and my preaching were not in persuasive words of wisdom, but in demonstration of the Spirit and of power* (1 Corinthians 2:4).

With the Holy Spirit as our Guide and the Scriptures as our plumb line, Jesus will lead us safely through this transition into a broad place. Get ready for change...get ready for revolution—a spiritual one.

# Chapter One

# A CALL FOR REVOLUTION

S hirley Ross, our program producer, had been viewing some footage of an interview that she wanted to use for one of our shows during the upcoming season when she came upon something very troubling. "Patricia, take a look at this!" she said with an air of astonishment. An ex-satanist was disclosing the most grueling details of her past involvement in cultic life.

Her name was Rebecca. As a young child, nannies from a satanic cult had taught her the black arts, and by the age of four, she had learned things like how to move objects without touching them. In addition, she had been violated by the high priest of the coven every day, who also made her take a demonic counterfeit of the communion rite that Christians observe. She testified that she was forced daily to drink a concoction of blood, urine, semen, and a black widow spider. She claimed to have operated in satanic power in order to control fire, to work false signs and wonders through spells, and she even disclosed information about animal and human sacrifice. The footage produced right-eous fury within me.

The enemy is running rampant with deception and pernicious evil in these days, and multitudes are caught in the grasp of his tactics. Who is going to stop him? And who will rescue those who are trapped in his evil snares? We need a spiritual revolution!

I was reminded of a personal trip to Africa in the 1980s with my husband, Ron. At that time, we met a number of Christians who testified concerning their life in satanic cults prior to coming to the Lord. They shared how they had walked through walls, flown in the spirit from one destination to another, changed into animal forms and back again, and how they had conjured up thousands of dollars at a time by performing satanic rituals.

We also heard stories of how hard-core satanists and witches were skilled in casting curses during destruction rites and how they would infiltrate churches, posing as Christians, and establish themselves in leadership circles and positions in attempt to thwart and destroy the purposes of God.

This type of scenario was not foreign to me. While laboring on the mission field in Central America, we were aware of satanic covens and their operations. A well-known witch in one village would levitate to the top of three-story buildings, and she would continually attempt to cast debilitating curses on the Christian workers. Unfortunately, although most Christians walked in a measure of divine protection, we did see some of these curses land on and affect some people. Although we are not to be afraid of any demonic powers, we do need to deliberately appropriate the pro-tective covering that is found in Christ. All the promises of God belong to every believer, but in order for them to be realized in a Christian's experience, they must be intentionally appropriated by faith. We are in a raging battle and we must be alert, walking in wisdom with our full armor secured.

A shift toward the use of demonic crafts is all too common in our day, and there are camps of individuals within satanic covens who deliberately challenge Christian authority in the spirit. A young person confessed in a television interview recently that when she was in a satanic cult, she "hated Christians because they were so weak, so powerless."

My blood boils at the very thought of this evil counterfeit power mocking God's people and running unchecked in the earth. My soul is vexed with this travesty. We desperately need God's mighty power to be unleashed in the church!

## God Will Not Be Mocked

Throughout the history of the Hebrew people, we see periods when it appears that satanic forces had overpowered the saints. Sadly, these occasions were usually attached to periods when Israel was walking in disobedience to the will of God. I especially think of Israel in the days of Moses; the people of God were greatly oppressed spiritually, economically, and politically by the Egyptians who ruled over them. Egypt was full of idolatry and sorcery—wicked forces that were integrated into the fabric of the Egyptian culture. They continuously taunted and abused God's people until the oppressed Hebrews finally cried out in the midst of their bondage; and as a result of their cries, the Lord provided them a deliverer.

His name was Moses. As a baby, his life had been miraculously spared from death, and he was brought into Pharaoh's household. Moses was then raised as an Egyptian and heavily influenced by their religious and political culture. Obviously, he would have been familiar with the Hermetic secrets that established the order of the Egyptian priesthood and religious practices in those days, and he would have seen the practice of the black arts by these Egyptian priests. In addition, Pharaoh's courts were frequented by magicians and sorcerers attempting to impress the leaders and people with their spiritual power and authority. The political leaders trusted in their abilities, while most of the people were afraid of them.

Eventually, after discovering his true identity and then slaying an Egyptian, Moses fled into the desert where he remained until God confronted him in the burning bush. In Exodus 4:1-9, we are invited to listen in as God converses with Moses about his return to Egypt and God's plan to rescue His people. At this point, Moses is very doubtful that the Egyptians will listen to him. So, God gives a demonstration to Moses, explaining to him that it will be through signs and wonders that He will free His people.

The first command He gives to Moses is to throw down his staff. As he does so, it becomes a serpent, and in verse 3, the Scripture informs us that Moses flees. I somehow don't believe this was because he was afraid of natural serpents. As a keeper of flocks in Midian, he would have seen serpents, lizards, and desert dragons on a regular basis, and would have beaten them off with his shepherd's rod. Instead, I believe that Moses was afraid of the magical art of sorcery associated with his past. Turning a rod into a serpent was something he had probably seen the sorcerers do in Pharoah's court with their intimidating magic power. And now, he was personally witnessing God's holy power produce a miracle that resembled what he had observed growing up. He was afraid of witchcraft and consequently was confused and frightened by what was transpiring before him, as many Christians are today.

## Witchcraft or God's Supernatural Power?

God then instructed Moses to take the serpent up by the tail—the most dangerous way to pick up a serpent. Moses, however, obeyed God, and immediately the serpent turned back into a rod. Through this miracle, God demonstrated to Moses that a standard was being raised up against the sorcerers who had controlled God's people with fear and intimidation. The miracle was a sign—a supernatural sign that God was going to deliver His people.

The Lord continued to instruct Moses: *"'Now put your hand into your bosom.' So, [Moses] put his hand into his bosom, and when he took it out, behold his hand was leprous like snow. Then He said, 'Put your hand into your bosom again.' So he put his hand into his bosom again, and when he took it out of his bosom, behold, it was restored like the rest of his flesh"* (Exod. 4:6-7).

The third sign and wonder that the Lord spoke to Moses involved taking water from the Nile and pouring it out on the land. It would then turn to blood (see Exod. 4:9). Once again, this would not have been a peculiar sight for Moses. He had seen the sorcerers do many strange and powerful things. What was strange for him, however, was to actually work these miracles himself by the power of a holy God who had just visited him in the burning bush, a God who identified Himself as I AM (see Exod. 3:14).

## Source Is a Factor

To discern whether a work is from God or not, you must test it against God's Word and align it with His character in an effort to expose the true source. Recently, I became aware of a Christian young person who had drifted away from God and was dabbling in a variety of witchcraft practices. He shared with me that by using the power of witchcraft, he could get any girl he wanted into bed with him within moments. He claimed, "All I have to do is exercise mind control." It is easy to test the validity of this act. It is completely contrary to God's Word, His ways, and His character; and therefore, this work can be discerned and disqualified immediately.

One of the differences between a sign or wonder worked by a sorcerer and a true miracle of God is the *source* of the power. The difference between a psychic and a true prophet of God is the *source*. In other words, from where do they receive their inspiration? Moses was called by God to work pure signs and wonders. Although they were similar to the types of miracles that the Egyptian sorcerers performed, there was an important difference—the source. While God's people were being oppressed, controlled, and intimidated by those who were operating in demonic power, He was now going to demonstrate His might through His chosen servant Moses by challenging the demonic forces that held His people captive.

James Goll, in his book, *The Seer*, offers some practical help on discerning the source of spiritual revelation and experiences.

> The Scriptures indicate that spiritual revelation or communication comes from any one of three sources: the Holy Spirit, the human soul, and the realm of evil spirits. The need for discernment in this area is obvious.
>
> *The Holy Spirit* is the only true source of revelation (see 2 Pet. 1:21). It was the Holy Spirit who moved the prophets of the Old Testament and the witnesses of the New Testament. The Greek word for "moved," *phero*, means "to be borne along" or even "to be driven along as a wind."

*The human soul* is capable of voicing thoughts, ideas, and inspirations out of the unsanctified portion of our emotions (see Ezek. 13:1-6; Jer. 23:16). These human inspirations are not necessarily born of God. As Ezekiel the prophet said, they are prophecies "out of their own hearts...Woe unto the foolish prophets, that follow their own spirit, and have seen nothing" (Ezek. 13:2-3 KJV).

*Evil spirits* operate with two characteristics common to their master. They can appear as "angels of light" (or as "good voices"), and they always speak lies because they serve the chief liar and the father of lies, satan. Messages delivered through evil spirits are often especially dangerous to people ignorant of God's Word or inexperienced in discernment because satan loves to mix just enough "truth" or factual statements in with his lies to trick gullible people. Just think of it as tasty bait carefully placed in the middle of a deadly trap. Acts 16:16-18 tells about a slave girl with a spirit of divination who *spoke the truth* about the disciples, but got it from a satanic source. When the apostle Paul eventually had heard enough and was irritated within, he commanded the spirit of divination to leave her.[1]

Oftentimes, Christians think that the difference between a demonic operation and a Christian work is simply the type or category of the operation. For instance, many might think that if the new-agers through deceptive powers are "astrotraveling" (the ability to project oneself from one location to another; to travel outside the body to another location), then it must be assumed that this type of spirit transport is demonic. Therefore, as Christians, we must never engage in this sort of demonic activity.

The problem with this thinking, however, is that the Bible shows evidence that God's people, such as Ezekiel, Elijah, Philip, and John, were empowered by the Holy Spirit in various levels of similar but very different spiritual transport in the invisible realm. The issue is not the type of act in most instances, but it is, in fact, the source of the act. Is it the Spirit of Christ initiating and empowering an act, or a demonic spirit, or perhaps even the carnal soul of man? All of God's works are pure, holy, righteous, and bear His fruit (see Gal. 5:22). This is the true source.

## God's Power Confrontations Through His People

Power confrontations are not unusual in the Bible. For example, we find Elijah challenging the prophets of Baal on Mount Carmel in First Kings chapter 18. God's people had been intimidated by Jezebel and the false prophets, and many had compromised their faith and followed Ahab and Jezebel into the worship of sexual deities such as Baal. Elijah arose in the midst of this intimidation and challenged the prophets of Baal through a power confrontation, calling them to work the same miracle as they called on their "power sources."

Having seen this type of spiritual operation before, they entered the challenge with confidence. However, this time was different. Elijah stood in the gap and hindered the demonic power from operating. The false prophets were caught off guard. A man was in their midst representing the true Power Source, the true and the living God, the Creator of all, the One with all authority and power, the One who is above all! Once again, in Bible history, we find God's power swallowing up the power of the enemy.

In the New Testament, we find Paul, during his first missionary journey, faced with spiritual opposition through a sorcerer named Elymas (see Acts 13:8). In the Scripture, we are not told exactly how Elymas opposed Paul as he was witnessing to the proconsul in Paphos, but it was not uncommon for sorcerers to use the demonic power of curses in attempt to thwart a Christian's assignment. When curses are released, Christian ministers often sense a great resistance and oppression in the unseen realm. This can oftentimes be very discouraging, causing ministers to shrink back. Paul, however, rose up in faith, operating in true Kingdom authority and God-power, and subsequently reversed the curse.

Being filled with the Holy Spirit, Paul firmly addressed the issue and then declared that Elymas would be blind for a season. Immediately, a mist and a darkness fell on the sorcerer, and as a result, the proconsul came to know Jesus (see Acts 13:11-12).

This was a power confrontation against the occult forces. The ultimate end of this encounter was that Jesus Christ was glorified as the One who indeed holds all power and authority. If Paul had not risen up to operate in true Kingdom authority and the demonstration of Christ's power, then the demonic power would have prevailed unchecked. The Church must not abdicate its position of exercising true Kingdom power and authority.

Today, many believers shrink back from the possibilities of supernatural experiences that are Holy Spirit filled and directed because they have heard of witches performing similar counterfeit acts. Many Christians today are actually frightened of the spiritual and the supernatural as a result.

I believe there are times when God supernaturally manifests Himself through His people in a way that is judged by some to be demonic. For example, many of our evangelical brothers have mistakenly thought that the gift of tongues being exercised in the church today is inspired by demonic influence. However, just because we do not understand spiritual phenomenon does not mean that it is demonic. Unfortunately, we often too quickly judge what we do not understand.

God will manifest Himself in supernatural ways for His people, and when some hear about such unexplainable acts, they will panic and judge the experience as demonically sourced simply because they have heard that similar things to these are practiced in the new age and the occult. Never forget that the devil is an imitator and will attempt to copy the works and acts of God. We must always remember that the enemy is a counterfeit, and his sleight of hand, supernatural imitations are simply flash and fraud.

The difference between the counterfeit and the true is not necessarily found in the act itself but is found in source, motive, and character. Satan is a fallen angel who was cast out of Heaven by God because corruption was found in him. *"You were blameless in your ways from the day you were created until unrighteousness was found in you"* (Ezek. 28:15). *"How you have fallen from heaven, O star of the morning, son of the dawn! You have been cut down to the earth, you who have weakened the nations!"* (Isa. 14:12).

The source of the devil's works is evil and corrupt just like him. The Bible teaches us not to follow him or his instructions in any way. Remember that Jesus did tell us that satan has come to steal, kill, and destroy. His motivation is to deceive and to destroy—quite different from the Father's motivation, which is to reveal and heal.

The enemy will always attempt to counterfeit the true. He always has. He lusts for power and position in the earth. Meanwhile, the Church is to be expressing and demonstrating the true so that the masses will be able to discern the difference and make right choices as a result. James Goll offers nine tests that enables one to discern the source of a revelation or experience and its accuracy and validity.

1. Does the revelation edify, exhort, or console?

2. Is it in agreement with God's Word?

3. Does it exalt Jesus Christ?

4. Does it have good fruit?

5. If it predicts a future event, does it come to pass?

6. Does the prophetic prediction turn people toward God (Jesus Christ) or away from Him?

7. Does it produce liberty or bondage?

8. Does it produce life or death?

9. Does the Holy Spirit bear witness that it is true?[2]

When I was a child, my mother served us inexpensive margarine (a butter substitute) because our family was unable to afford real butter. I had always eaten margarine and did not realize there was a difference between it and butter until I was introduced to the real thing. Oh my, I can actually remember tasting real butter for the first time. It was so good, so rich, and so very different. When I went back to margarine, I longed for butter, the real deal made directly from the cream of milk, while margarine, made from vegetable oil and flavored with milk, is a poor substitute.

In my mind, there is no contest. Butter wins hands down. In like manner, if the world only knows of counterfeit power, they never realize the true spiritual power whose source comes from God. But, when they taste of the higher and truer power, there is no contest...there is no comparison!

When we do not operate in the true power of God, the enemy gains the advantage and fills the void left by the church. We must take this position back.

In the days of Moses, God's covenant people had not stood in their God-given mandate to follow Jehovah, and as a result, they became oppressed by their enemies. They were called to be the head and not the tail, above and not beneath, but they forgot who they were. They disobeyed God and subsequently were ruled by an oppressor. Then it came time for Israel to be restored to God. It was time for Pharaoh to let God's people go. It was time for a power confrontation!

When Moses and Aaron went into Pharaoh's courts, Aaron threw the rod of Moses down and it became a serpent. After this, *"Pharaoh also called for the wise men and the sorcerers, and they also, the magicians of Egypt, did the same with their secret arts. For each one threw down his staff and they turned into serpents. But Aaron's staff swallowed up their staffs"* (Exod. 7:11-12).

This example clearly teaches us that we need to exercise true Kingdom power and authority in order to swallow up the false power and authority of the enemy. Moses and Aaron were performing the same acts that were common to the sorcerers in their day. For years, the operation of these demonic acts were allowed to function in the land unchecked, and until Moses, no one had had taken a stand against these powers. No challenge had been made. Now, God was instructing Moses to demonstrate true power and authority that when exercised would ultimately bring freedom to a nation held captive to the demonic strongholds. The supernatural miracles, signs, and wonders performed by Moses not only confronted the demonically inspired acts but turned the attention of the Hebrews back to their God. The supernatural acts performed by the Spirit of the Lord through Moses caused Egypt to eventually tremble in the realization that the God of the Hebrews was indeed God of all, and their false beliefs were no match for this awesome God.

As Bill Johnson shares in his book, *When Heaven Invades Earth*, expectations grow when people are exposed to the power of God. "The testimony of God creates an appetite for more of the activities of God. Expectation grows wherever people are mindful of His supernatural nature and covenant. When the expectation grows, miracles increase. When the miracles increase, testimonies increase as well. You can see the cycle. The simple act of sharing a testimony about God can stir up others until they expect and see God work in their day."[3]

The Lord is raising up a standard today against the false expressions of the enemy in our land by stirring His people to demonstrate the true power of our God. We are about to see the Church rise up today in amazing confrontational authority and power. Like Moses in the midst of Egypt, like Elijah in the midst of the prophets of Baal, like Daniel in the midst of Babylon, like Jesus in the midst of religious strongholds, and like Paul in the midst of persecution, the Lord is raising up His people today to work true signs and wonders that will capture the attention of the world as it brings healing and deliverance to those who are sick and oppressed. These true signs and wonders will be the standard raised up against the flood of the counterfeit demonic outpouring. We must walk in the true in order to expose and swallow up the false.

Like Moses, we will see God's power swallow up the enemy's power. Like Elijah, we will see false prophets bow to the true and living God declaring, "The Lord, He is God. The Lord, He is God."

## Churchianity or Kingdom?

In Second Timothy 3:5, Paul warns concerning a people in the last days who will hold to *"a form of godliness but deny its power."*

Are we in danger of this circumstance in our day? Most services in the Western church are very predictable. We gather, often on a Sunday morning, and are usually welcomed at the door by "greeters." As we enter the building, it is normal to be handed a bulletin, and we take our seat in a church sanctuary or auditorium. The leader opens the meeting, and the praise and worship begins. After about 40 minutes to an hour, the singing ends, and announcements and offerings are received. A message is given usually by a pastor, and then often there is an invitation for people to receive prayer at the closing of the service. Following the dismissal, many people quickly exit the building to enjoy their Sunday chicken dinner.

I am not saying that this church-going pattern is necessarily wrong, and I definitely don't believe that we are to abandon the gathering together of believers for worship, equipping, fellowship, and accountability. I am saying, though, that this in itself is not the fullness of the Kingdom. In First Corinthians 2:4, we find Paul explaining that the Kingdom of God does not consist of persuasive words of man's wisdom but with a demonstration of the Holy Spirit and of the power of God so that our faith would not rest in words only, but in power.

For the most part, we have been completely comfortable with a powerless church. We are satisfied with a cranial and academic orientation that denies the supernatural. But where did we receive this model from? Or where in the Bible can we find it?

Too often we deny the supernatural and settle for religious activity and structure. Instead, we must come to know our God as a God of power, because He is! Jesus came to not only teach concerning the Kingdom but to demonstrate the Kingdom in which Jesus Himself is the King and holds all authority in Heaven and in earth. We must come to understand His Kingdom in its fullness and truly walk as His people in the realm of the supernatural.

## A New Spiritual Era

The masses today are increasingly intrigued by and hungry for spiritual things. An emphasis on materialism, career, and education in our society, for the most part, has left them feeling empty and longing for purpose in life. The youth of today are generally fearful of the future and yet are longing to give themselves to something meaningful. They often feel powerless next to the shakings around them.

As a result, growing numbers are turning to a variety of things that they hope will grant them a sense of security. Some have turned to drugs in an attempt to experience either a feeling of empowerment or an illusive rest from all the pressures that invade their peace. Yet the drug scene with its smorgasbord of choices has left many in this generation broken, disillusioned, and without hope.

Others are attempting to find their well-being through sexual fulfillment. Sexual promiscuity, perversion, and confusion in sexual orientation have increased greatly in these days partly due to the fact that people are longing for deep and meaningful relationships. Instead of this goal being realized, however, many have been left shipwrecked, wounded, and violated.

This generation is seeking for something they can live for, something they can die for. Yet, education, family, career, material security, sexual fulfillment, church life, and escapism through the drug scene—these all have fallen short in satisfying the deep inner cries resident in most hungry hearts. Political activists have failed in offering national and global security; military forces are vulnerable; economic systems are shaky, and even the earth itself is regularly trembling with an increased frequency of earthquakes and natural disasters. As a result, we are seeing a growing emergence of spiritual hunger and awakening.

A church-going mentality has no appeal to these ones who are desperately spiritually hungry. Why would it? If they simply want to attend meetings, there are many good-will organizations in every community that they can join.

People everywhere are hungry for power and are consequently turning to the supernatural, and spiritual cults are increasing rapidly as the masses look for a power that is greater than themselves. An individual in the United Nations predicted at the turn of the millennium that the greatest commodity of this century would be the spirituality of man. The most popular, best-selling books in the early part of the millennium has been *Harry Potter*, a series about a young sorcerer. Bookstores can barely keep them in stock when they first hit the shelves. People are hungry for the manifestation of unseen, spiritual power.

Man is a spiritual being and deep inside he understands that there is a realm, a reality, and a dimension that is beyond him and of which he is a part. Unfortunately, religion of the 21st century and its parched, spiritless theology has very little to offer the modern man who seeks a spirituality that is high above the rationalism of our day.

## Signs of This Transition Are Everywhere

Consequently, we have now entered an era of transition. Signs of this transition are everywhere, and Christians must discern them. Movies, television programs, books, and other expressions of media are full of the supernatural. It is not unusual to observe a psychic, a witch, warlock, ghost, spirit medium, or someone operating in supernatural power on television daily.

The music industry, in addition, is promoting sounds of the spirit world. New Age doctrine has infiltrated the education system, the medical profession, the political realm, law enforcement systems, and the business world. Spiritual super-heroes are being introduced through various media, drawing affections and imaginations toward deliverers who promise release and relief. Children's television programs, cartoons, and games are also often supernatural in nature.

And where is the Church in the midst of this counterfeit uprising? Where is the demonstration of God's power in and through His people? Outside of a small remnant of hungry Christians, there are very few in the Western church who actually adhere to the teaching in the Scriptures concerning God's operative power through believers today. And a sadder reality than this is, of those who believe that God's power is real today, very few are actually operating in much of it at all, including myself!

How can we, the Church of the living God, sit back and watch the enemy deceive with false signs, wonders, and miracles? How can we be complacent and powerless at such a critical time in history? It is time to arise in the fullness of His grace and in the manifestation of the true righteous power of the Kingdom. It is time to bring forth a spiritual revolution.

Oh, that Christians would be at least half as diligent in seeking God's presence and power as the satanists are in seeking demonic authority. As in the days of Moses, are there believers who will raise the standard and manifest the true in the midst of the false today?

It is imperative at this critical hour that we dedicate ourselves afresh to seeking the face of the Lord and to becoming familiar with scriptural teaching concerning the invisible Kingdom realm. It is vital that we allow the Holy Spirit to lead us into heavenly and supernatural perspectives that we possibly have not been comfortable with up to this time. Some of these insights will be introduced initially with a measure of wrestling and resistance in the hearts of believers. Therefore, we need to learn to discern. In John 3:12, Jesus spoke to Nicodemus, a ruler of the Jews, and said, *"If I told you earthly things and you do not believe, how will you believe if I tell you heavenly things?"*

We will be hearing of increased numbers of testimonies regarding believers engaging in spiritual experiences such as those we have read about in the Bible. Appearances of Jesus, angelic visitation, traveling in the realm of the spirit, throne room experiences, dreams, visions, trances, walking through walls, miracles, signs, wonders, and supernatural phenomena are occurring much more frequently. There are spiritual insights that will be introduced to the Church in the coming days that up to this time our *"eye hath not seen, nor ear heard, neither have entered into the heart of man, the things which God hath prepared for them that love Him"* (1 Cor. 2:9 KJV).

Paul continues in verse 10 to say that the Lord will reveal these things to us by His Spirit. In John 16:12-13, Jesus said to His disciples, *"I have many more things to say to you, but you cannot bear them now. But when He, the Spirit of truth, comes, He will guide you into all the truth; for He will not speak on His own initiative, but whatever He hears, He will speak; and He will disclose to you what is to come."*

It is vital then, that we, the Church, press in to know, love, and exalt God with all our hearts and lives. It is equally vital that we honor and submit to the Holy Spirit, diligently study the Word of God, discover what is rightfully ours in Christ, and lead the way into this new era of awareness of spiritual sensitivity and Kingdom reality. Again, how will we ever learn to discern the counterfeit if we are not familiar with the *real thing*? How will the unsaved ever embrace the truth if they know only the false?

## One Savior, One Lord, and One Glorious and Eternal King

There is one Savior, one Lord, and one glorious and eternal King—Jesus Christ the righteous! His ways are unsearchable. His glory is magnificent. His power is unparalleled. His love is unfailing. His wisdom is beyond comprehension. Oh, what a truly awesome God we serve!

My passion in writing this book is to awaken hunger in believers for all that Scripture offers in the area of God-encounters, deep intimacy with Jesus, and authentic Kingdom experience in His glory and power. Valid spiritual experience and enhanced spiritual sensitivity are awaiting believers in this hour. May we become comfortable with biblical terms and concepts such as, signs and wonders, Third Heaven, throne room, heavenly places, angels, living creatures around the throne, the great cloud of witnesses, rainbows, glory clouds, heavenly colors and gems, spirit transport, dreams, visions, heavenly fragrances, miracles, heavenly languages, divine healings, cleansing of lepers, resurrection of the dead, and casting out of demons—all the normal Kingdom stuff! The Lord desires to open our spiritual eyes to see, our ears to hear and to understand things that we possibly have not even dreamt of yet in our wildest imaginations. His Kingdom is vast and magnificent, full of power, authority, and every good thing. He wants us to explore and experience this realm with Him.

## Live From a Heavenly Perspective

We will definitely need to live from a heavenly perspective in these last days. There will be great turmoil and treachery in the earth, but we, the glorious Church, are to live our lives from a different viewpoint than those without Christ. We are to be a people who are focused on the heavenly, the divine, and the supernatural. We are to be a people who demonstrate His Kingdom authority and power. We are to set our affections upon Him! He is the sole object of our worship and our trust. *"Therefore if you have been raised up with Christ, keep seeking the things above, where Christ is, seated at the right hand of God"* (Col. 3:1). Jesus Christ is the source of true power and authority. He is the One who sits in the heavens far above all principality, power, and rule. His power is matchless. His authority is eternally established. His love is amazing! Let us be a people who pursue Him, who love Him, who adore Him, and for the sake of His glory in the earth, let us be a people who embrace this spiritual revolution.

## Endnotes

1. Jim W. Goll, *The Seer* (Shippensburg, PA: Destiny Image Publishers, 2004), 73-74.

2. Ibid., 76-78.

3. Bill Johnson, *When Heaven Invades Earth* (Shippensburg, PA: Destiny Image Publishers, 2004), 121.

Chapter Two

# Spiritual Experiences— Are They Valid?

Have you ever imagined yourself eating and drinking with God on sapphire streets, or entering a glorious cloud of His Presence; gazing at the Lord high on His throne while His kingly train fills the temple, or personally encountering angels? Have you ever, in your wildest dreams, contemplated the possibilities of literally outrunning chariots like Elijah did in First Kings 18:46 when *"the hand of the Lord was on Elijah"*; or observing the armies of Heaven in action in Second Kings 6:17—*"Then Elisha prayed and said, 'O Lord, I pray, open his eyes that he may see.' And the Lord opened the servant's eyes, and he saw; and behold, the mountain was full of horses and chariots of fire all around Elisha"*; or walking through walls like Jesus did—*"So when it was evening on that day, the first day of the week, and when the doors were shut where the disciples were, for fear of the Jews, Jesus came and stood in their midst and said to them, 'Peace be with you'"* (John 20:19)?

How about being supernaturally transported from one geographical location to another by the Spirit of God like Philip was? *"When they came up out of the water, the Spirit of the Lord snatched Philip away; and the eunuch no longer saw him, but went on his way rejoicing"* (Acts 8:39).

Dare we permit the Lord, should He desire, to fill our lives with God-directed and inspired supernatural occurrences as we find in the scriptural examples just mentioned? And if we were to do so, what purpose would this serve?

How could supernatural visions, seeing an angel, or hanging out in the "throne zone" enhance our worship and devotion of the King of kings in any way? How could such experiences possibly make us stronger Christians, and deepen our intimacy with Jesus? How could such possibilities make us better witnesses for the Lord in this hour of awakened spirituality?

Throughout the Scripture, we find that such encounters are not only possible in a believer's experience, should the Holy Spirit lead in that way, but that the Lord actually desires us to participate with Him in supernatural Kingdom life.

Many believers in Christ are absolutely desperate to experience the Lord and His Kingdom in tangible and meaningful ways. They are longing to experience intimacy with Jesus, to behold His glory, and to stand in His presence. During a spiritual revolution, many believers will identify within themselves an insatiable hunger to experience in real ways the God of all power. They will be passionate in their pursuit of supernatural visitation.

## Is Desire for "God-Experiences" Valid?

Many are concerned and opposed to what is often referred to as "experience orientation." James and Michal Ann Goll, in their book, *God Encounters*, offer some great reasons why these giftings are important: "to apprehend us and cause us to better see this glorious man Jesus Christ; to awaken in us a desire to know Him more intimately; to stir up within us a hunger and thirst for Him that we may scarcely have been aware of. The entire purpose of revelatory giftings is to spur us into greater pursuit of Him."[1]

For the most part, the phrase "experience orientation" is understood to refer to those who have a passionate pursuit of God-given experiences: His gifts, His presence, and His activity. Although I agree that we are to be careful not to worship "experience," I would like to gently and respectfully challenge this concern.

Successful and meaningful relationships are based on a choice to love as well as to experience that love. If you were to take the experience dimension out of a relationship, you would more than likely be left with a cold and empty association and not a relationship at all. If you were to read the biography of the President of the United States, it doesn't mean that you have a relationship with him. It simply means you know something about him. If you had coffee with him, however, or went for a walk with him, or allowed him to take you on a personal tour of the White House, then you could perhaps say that you had a small measure of relationship with him. What makes the difference? It is the experience dimension. The more experience you share with someone, the deeper your relationship becomes.

Here is an example: Imagine a bridegroom standing at the altar, with heart pounding, waiting to make a life commitment to his bride who is walking down the aisle toward him, arrayed in her elaborate bridal apparel and appearing more ravishing than he has ever seen her. He is "experiencing" intense waves of passionate love and anticipation washing over his emotions. After she finally makes her way to the front of the church and stands beside him in all of her bridal radiance, they begin to say their vows. She looks at the groom with sincerity during this moment of sealing a lifelong covenant and says tenderly and with conviction, "I vow to be your wife, to be faithful to you, to submit to you...but don't expect to *experience* my love. I'm not into experience. I don't want our marriage to be based on experience. Oh...and I don't expect to feel your love either. I will simply believe that you love me. I will stand faithfully on the words of this covenant every day, but I will not expect, nor will I pursue experience in our relationship."

Oh my, what a disappointment to the bridegroom. Perhaps he will change his mind right there at the altar. Why? Because experience has everything to do with relationship. It is impossible to enjoy a rich, passionate, and meaningful relationship without experience. Experience is absolutely essential. Of course, a healthy balance is based on an unshakable, quality decision to commit to the relationship and to love the person deeper than you would love any experience. You actually cannot have one without the other in order to live in a flourishing Kingdom relationship. You must give unconditional commitment as well as provide experience when expressing love. Love needs to be expressed and received in order for it to operate.

As we mentioned previously, you cannot really become acquainted with the qualities of a person simply by reading a biography about him or her. You come to know them only by spending time with them—communicating, listening, and interacting. This is also how it works in our walk with the Lord. He desires to know us intimately, and for us to know Him just as deeply. He desires us to experience His love, His kindness, and His truth; and He longs to experience our love as well. He would be so disappointed if we said, "Reading the Bible is all I need. I can find everything I need to know about You, Lord, through Your Word. It doesn't matter to me if I experience Your love, presence, or power." This would break His heart, for He longs to give us experience with Him and to receive our love as well. He is a relational God. When He was suffering on the cross, He had an expectation. He endured the cross for the joy set before Him. Experiencing an eternal love relationship with you is that joy.

## The Lord Desires Us to Experience His Kingdom

Not only are we invited to experience the Lord Himself, but He also desires us to experience His Kingdom. I am a Canadian and have lived most of my life in North American culture. I am Canadian because I was born in Canada, and I have a birth certificate to prove it. It is the daily experiences in my nation and culture, however, that has actually caused me to be Canadian in lifestyle, appearance, language, and personality. I have experienced Canadian culture for years and, therefore, act and function as a Canadian. This North American flair did not come from studying the Canadian Constitution; it came through daily *experience* in Canadian culture. The laws of our land definitely form and shape the perimeters of acceptable activity within our nation, but it is actually the experience within that framework that gives my fellow Canadians the noted "Canadian personality."

I have traveled into many nations and noticed that there are distinct characteristics among cultures and peoples. I am able, in most cases, to tell the difference between an American and a Canadian or between someone from Germany and someone from Holland even though these nations are located right next to each other. I can usually tell the difference between an African-American with Nigerian heritage and a Nigerian who was born and raised in Africa. Experience and life in their culture and environment causes the primary distinction.

It is the same for us as children of God. The Lord desires us to fully experience His Kingdom. As we do so, we begin to take on the profile of a *Kingdom citizen*. Our citizenship in this glorious eternal dominion is first secured once we accept Jesus Christ as our Savior, and as a Kingdom child, there are many blessings and benefits that are then granted us. In this domain, we find the sovereign Lord governing over the universe and we become acquainted with the glory of His presence, power, and His majesty. We are invited to behold Him and His wonderful love. There is so much to discover.

There is a real place called *Heaven* within this Kingdom. There are angels, chariots, fiery ones around the throne, a crystal sea, a river of life, the tree of life, the great cloud of witnesses, golden streets, and oh...so much more! The Word of God is full of information and revelation regarding the Kingdom of God, and we have been invited to discover and partake of it all.

As we experience on a daily basis this glorious Kingdom life, then we will take on Kingdom characteristics, Kingdom language, and Kingdom activity.

> *Do not be afraid, little flock, for your Father has chosen gladly to give you the Kingdom* (Luke 12:32).

> *But seek first His kingdom and His righteousness, and all these things will be added to you* (Matthew 6:33).

## Whom or What Do We Seek?

Someone addressed me once with a word of warning after I had shared in a conference about the glory of the heavenly realm. He said, "Sister Patricia, you need to be careful not to get the focus of the brothers and sisters off the face of Jesus. They must seek only His face and not His hands or His truth or His gifts." He addressed a number of other concerns he had, and I listened carefully. I think it is healthy and helpful for us to listen to the thoughts of others and weigh them, even if at the end of the process you choose not to agree. It is wise to be a thoughtful listener, to be teachable, and approach opposition with a spirit of humility.

I fully believe that the person and presence of the Lord Himself should be the most important focus of our attention. Absolutely! I also believe that we are to love Him with all our heart. Something this gentleman said, however, didn't quite settle well within me even though I understood the general point he was trying to state. As I inquired of the Lord, I was given this little scenario: I saw a vision of a mother standing in her kitchen. In front of her was her little girl. They were facing each other, and the mother said, "Honey, I baked your favorite cookies today. They are over there on the counter, and I want you to help yourself. I made them just for you." The little girl, who appeared to be around ten years old in the vision replied, "No, Mommy! No, Mommy! I don't want any cookies. I only want your face. I love your face, Mommy, and I only want to look at your face! No cookies."

The mother looked rather shocked but gently answered, "Sweetie, I am so glad that you love me, and I am really happy that you like my face, but I want you to enjoy a cookie. I made them especially for you."

"No, Mommy, no! No cookie. Nothing from your hand. Only your face."

By this time, Mommy was really concerned and with sternness said, "Child, go get a cookie and stop this nonsense."

Now, in the natural, if this were to actually happen, we would think the child needed some serious counseling for her unbalanced behavior. Children are to feel a sense of belonging and enjoyment in their home environment, and when a parent gives his child a gift or an object of provision, it is expected that the child will receive it with joy and thankfulness. When I give my grandson a gift (which is every time I visit), I am thrilled when he enjoys it. He loves his Gramma King and is always glad to see me. We have a beautiful bond of love between us. But while he loves me, he also enjoys the things I give him...and I want him to.

So it is with the Lord. We are to love Him in a deep and personal way, but we are also to enjoy the things He has prepared for us. *"He who did not spare His own Son, but delivered Him over for us all, how will He not also with Him freely give us all **things**?"* (Rom. 8:32, emphasis added).

How many times do we find believers behaving before the Lord in the same way as the young girl did before her mother? I agree with Bob Mumford who often said, "God called us to be childlike, not childish."

Thinking that we are being noble and highly spiritual, we may stand before the Lord and say, "No, Lord, not Your hand. Only Your face, only Your face. No blessings. No angels. No glory manifestations. No power. No gifts. Only Your face!" We carry on like this and don't realize that we are living in major spiritual dysfunction. This is not normal behavior for a healthy relationship.

It is important for us to be fully in love with the person of Jesus Christ, our Savior and Lord, but it is equally important to enjoy the benefits of that relationship. The things that are given to us by His hand are an expression of His love for us. As we engage in experience with Jesus and the things He has freely given us, our relationship will deepen and become greatly enhanced.

It is so easy to love God when you understand and know His love for you. Loving Him is not something we should have to force ourselves to do. *"We love Him, because He first loved us"* (1 John 4:19 KJV). The more we understand His goodness, the easier it is to love Him. How can you not? It is even His goodness that calls us out of darkness to follow after Him. *"Or do you think lightly of the riches of His kindness and tolerance and patience, not knowing that the kindness of God leads you to repentance?"* (Rom. 2:4).

The Lord has invited us into a real Kingdom that is full of power and limitless measures of blessing. *"Blessed be the God and Father of our Lord Jesus Christ, who has blessed us with every spiritual blessing in the heavenly places in Christ"* (Eph. 1:3).

Although it is an invisible Kingdom that we were born into, it is still a very real Kingdom. *"While we look not at the things which are seen, but at the things which are not seen; for the things which are seen are temporal, but the things which are not seen are eternal"* (2 Cor. 4:18).

There are many things in the unseen Kingdom realm. There truly are angels, glory clouds, chariots, chariot drivers, spirit horses, living creatures, gemstones, thunder, lightning, radiant colors, lakes, rivers, trees, bowls of incense, and all sorts of other things in this Kingdom. And guess what? We are to seek these *things*. Yes, that is right! Not only are we to seek Jesus, but we are to actually *seek* the *things* of the Kingdom—the things of the unseen realm.

*Therefore if you have been raised up with Christ, keep seeking the things above, where Christ is, seated at the right hand of God. **Set your mind on the things** above,* *not on the things that are on earth* (Colossians 3:1-2, emphasis added).

Isn't this interesting? We are actually exhorted to seek the *things* above where Christ is seated. We will go into this aspect more in another chapter when we talk about the Third Heaven, but for now it is enough for us to know that we are to seek the things above. If we are to be people in pursuit of His power, we need to not only be seekers of the God of power Himself but also of the things in the Kingdom that He created by His great power.

In Colossians 3:1-2, Paul doesn't only suggest that the believers at Colossae should seek the face of Jesus. Of course, they were to seek the *face* of Jesus, but Paul also emphasized the fact that they were to *seek the things above where Christ is seated.* We need to seek Him heart-to-heart on a regular basis, but we also need to seek other things in His Kingdom that He wants us to embrace in our experience. There are *things* in the heavenly and unseen dimension that He wants us to enjoy, so much so, that the Scriptures say we are to actually seek these *"things."*

I desire to draw as close to the Lord as possible. I pursue Him daily. I want as much Kingdom experience in my life as possible. I constantly believe for more of God, for more of the reality of His Kingdom to be made known to me, for more embracing of the *things* He has created for me to enjoy, and for more of His manifest power. And do you know what? He loves it when I ask for more. You can too. Go for it!

Experience orientation is valid if it has a place of right priority within your heart. Experience, for the sake of experience, however, has no eternal value at all, and the idolatry of it could possibly lead to great deception. Experience in knowing Him, His Kingdom, and His righteousness, however, is our upward call in Christ Jesus.

*But whatever things were gain to me, those things I have counted as loss for the sake of Christ. ...That I may know Him and the power of His resurrection and the fellowship of His sufferings, being conformed to His death. ...Brethren, I do not regard myself as having laid hold of it yet; but one thing I do: forgetting what lies behind and reaching forward to what lies ahead, I press on toward the goal for the prize of the upward call of God in Christ Jesus* (Philippians 3:7,10,13-14, emphasis added).

## Days of Tumult and Tension

Throughout the Scriptures, we discover that most of the supernatural empowerments of God were witnessed during days of great tumult and tension. On the other hand, when peace was in the land, you will not find too much written in the Scriptures regarding God's mighty works and displays of His power. Moses lived in days of great oppression, and yet he experienced many awesome acts in the presence of the Lord. Elijah, Elisha, Daniel, David, Jeremiah, Ezekiel, and Isaiah, as well as Christ's disciples and the believers in the Book of Acts also witnessed and experienced many supernatural and divine occurrences. A great deal of space is given in the Scripture to all that God did during these times of pressure and trials, yet during seasons of peace, you might find a one-liner that goes something like this: *"So-and-so reigned for so many years, and there was peace in the land."*

Presently, we are headed into some treacherous days—days of great tumult and tension, days when men's hearts will turn to evil, being seduced by deceiving spirits and doctrines of demons. In fact, these days are already upon us. One afternoon, our Extreme Prophetic team was witnessing of Christ's love in an area of

Phoenix where many homeless people live. I met a young man that day who was about 17 or 18 years of age, who wore white opaque contact lenses with fine black lightning bolts coming out each side. No natural iris could be seen, only his black pupils with the white contacts threaded with black lightning. When he opened his mouth to respond to a question I asked, two long white fangs became evident. He had had dental implants inserted to give a Dracula appearance. It didn't take much to discern that he was steeped in some very dark spiritual stuff. We had some dialogue, and I gave some encouragement in the Lord. Following that encounter, I remained burdened for him.

Within 48 hours I had a spiritual encounter. I woke up from a sleep in the early morning and experienced something I was not expecting or asking for, but which was completely initiated by the Holy Spirit. In this visionary encounter, I found myself in a room looking at a young girl who appeared to be about 16 years of age and who looked very emaciated. I saw her very clearly. It appeared that she had just given birth, and her newborn son was lying on the bed she had given birth on. His cord had not yet been cut.

Also, in this vision, I saw the young man I had met on the street just two days earlier. I had a sense that he might be the father of the child, but one thing I knew for sure was that he was about to dedicate this baby to satan. In this spiritual vision, I laid my hands on the baby and prophesied his destiny in Christ. I named the name of Jesus over him as an act of dedication. I then came out of the visionary experience.

Oftentimes, the Lord will give experiences like this for the purpose of intercession, not for a specific situation, but for a certain people group. The people seen in this vision could have symbolically represented those caught up in the deceptive and destructive power of the occult. It is God's desire to intervene especially in the lives of children who are being abused by those involved in satanic witchcraft.

The world is full of confused and deceived people who are given over to great deceptions and trapped in demonic mind-sets. Isaiah prophesied in Isaiah 60:2 that darkness would cover the earth and deep darkness the people. Paul prophesied in his letter to Timothy that the "last days" would be treacherous days. *"But realize this, that in the last days difficult times will come"* (2 Tim. 3:1).

God is preparing us for what is ahead. During this season of spiritual revolution, He will teach us how to experience Him, His Kingdom, and His power in greater ways. We will arise and shine in the midst of the darkness and manifest the power and glory of God. Simply attending a service, conference, or engaging in a church program will no longer get us through the days ahead. We will need to know Him and experience Him like never before. We will definitely need to learn to walk and war as true Kingdom children, living in true Kingdom consecration, power, and grace.

In this treacherous hour, we can expect "God-encounters." The Bible is full of them. In fact, if you were to remove all the records of experience from the Bible and allowed only doctrine to remain, there would be very little left. And I emphasize that most biblical accounts of God-encounters, as I have already alluded to, were found in times of turmoil and tension. God's power is accelerated in such times.

## Open Our Eyes, Lord

The Scriptures reveal the reality of a God of power who desires His children to walk in the fullness of Kingdom life. In this treacherous hour, we must come out of the forms and mind-sets that have held us back from experiencing God, His power, and His Kingdom. We indeed need our eyes opened and our hearts enlarged to embrace all that the Lord wants to reveal to us.

Paul prayed to the Lord on behalf of the church at Ephesus, that they would receive *"a spirit of wisdom and of revelation in the knowledge of Him* [and] *that the eyes of your heart may be enlightened, so that you will know what is the hope of His calling, what are the riches of the glory of His inheritance in the saints, and what is the surpassing greatness of His power toward us who believe"* (Eph. 1:17-19). This same prayer is what we should echo today for the Church. This same prayer is what we can pray right now for ourselves. Let us go before the God of all power and invite Him to fill us.

> *Heavenly Father, I come before You in the name of Jesus and confess that I am hungry to know You, Your power, Your Kingdom, and Your righteousness. You said that those who hunger and thirst for righteousness shall be filled. Grant unto me a spirit of wisdom and revelation in the knowledge of You and open the eyes of My understanding to know Your ways. Grant me experiences with You—God-encounters. Grant me valid experiences in Your unseen Kingdom realm. Fill me with Your power that I might do the works of the Kingdom even as Jesus, Your Son did in the earth. Help me to feel comfortable living the life You have given me, by faith in Your Word. Make me an advocate for the spiritual revolution. Amen.*

## Endnote

1. James and Michal Ann Goll, *God Encounters* (Shippensburg, PA: Destiny Image Publishers, 2005), 170.

Chapter Three

# CATAPULTED
# INTO A NEW WINESKIN

My walk with the Lord has always been founded on a deep love and respect for the Word of God. I adore the Scriptures and make it my practice and discipline to immerse myself in them. As a young Christian, I was introduced to the person of the Holy Spirit and received instruction in His gifts, and the supernatural operation of the gifts of the Holy Spirit has been a normal occurrence in my life and ministry from the time I launched into full-time preaching and teaching in 1980. I have taught strong biblical foundations but have also allowed the Holy Spirit to flow in my personal life and in ministry meetings. At one point, I thought I was fairly cutting edge, and to be honest with you, I think I subconsciously believed that I had a handle on the operations of the Kingdom. This type of pride is very typical in historical revivals where the previous move of God has been found to persecute the next.

Early in my Christian walk, I earnestly prayed that the Lord would always "discipline me early." I cried out saying, "Lord, I never want to go to the right or the left of Your will. If I ever do, discipline me strong and immediately. Don't leave me to my own devices." So let's put it this way—I am a well disciplined child...oh my, am I ever! The disciplines, have taken various forms, and I must say that I am grateful for each and every one of them.

In 1980, the Lord brought forth great degrees of humility in my life by introducing me to new insights and manifestations of His glory that literally blew my mind! He revealed that His Kingdom was much larger and greater than I had ever known and beyond anything I could ever imagine. My friend, Charlie Robinson, often says, "When revival comes, it is never what you expect, but it is always better." I was about to discover this firsthand as the Lord taught me concerning the need of a new wineskin that would hold new wine. As a result, He shook my world! That is the kind of discipline I love. More, Lord!

## Heaven, Angels, Firebombs, and Laughter

"The wind of the Holy Spirit is about to blow upon this section of seating. Get ready, here He comes," declared the revivalist, just moments before the tangible blast of a powerful, holy wind struck our seating area. I was suddenly whacked with the glorious impact of this "wind power" and found myself crashing between two rows of metal chairs. But oh, how marvelous it all felt. There is nothing like a touch from the Holy Spirit! Before I could get a grip on what had just happened, the revivalist called for all those who felt the Spirit's power to make their way to the front. He believed the Spirit desired to touch us again.

I honestly did not know how I could possibly make it to the front because of the weakness I felt after the blast of power that overcame me, but I was determined to respond. I staggered forward and attempted to stand with others who were eagerly awaiting a second touch. Before another word was spoken, I fell down again under the power of the Spirit. This time I began to laugh loudly and uncontrollably!

My exuberant laughter in the midst of a public and solemn meeting embarrassed me, especially because I couldn't think of anything funny that would be triggering my response. And the more I attempted to arrest the hilarity, the worse it became. My mind and my heart began a wrestling match. My mind argued with the validity of such behavior while my heart delighted in the experience. A sincere question then rose from my spirit as I recall silently asking, "Lord, exactly what is so funny?" Then I burst into hilarity again. These uncontrollable outbursts merely increased my inner wrestling.

## I Heard Heaven Laughing

After numerous minutes of flailing on the floor and laughing explosively, the Lord in His goodness allowed me to enjoy a supernatural experience that I shall never forget. In a vision, I was taken into Heaven where I literally and audibly heard Heaven laughing. It sounded like an enormous multitude of voices exploding in such convulsive merriment that I thought someone had just told a good joke. Heaven's atmosphere appeared to be like that of a vibrant party. To be honest, this was disconcerting to me. I remember thinking, *Is this all you do up here—party and tell jokes while we are suffering greatly down on planet earth?* The Scripture says that the carnal flesh is at enmity against the Spirit (see Rom. 8:7). It is mind-boggling to think that you can be in Heaven and yet have thoughts that oppose God; just as lucifer, an archangel in the presence of God, where all was perfect, chose to accept wrong thoughts. Even so, despite my mental objections, my spirit was still enjoying Heaven's elation.

What amazed me was that every time Heaven laughed, I also laughed, and every time Heaven ceased, so would I. There seemed to be a divine connection between the laughter in Heaven and the laughter that was inspiring my spirit. I had no idea what was causing this intense release of joyful emotion, but it did feel very good! Heaven was completely filled with joy and without a trace of concern or anxiety. All was at peace! Everything felt wonderful! And the enormous weight of the glory caused my mental objections to be silent. Such contrary thoughts held no ground in such an atmosphere.

## Angels and Hot Coals

While in the midst of this sovereign heavenly encounter, I saw angels ascending from various locations on earth with coals in their hands. A large altar with a blazing fire appeared in the vision, on which the angels placed the coals they had brought from earth. Somehow I knew that these coals represented the prayers of the saints. In the fire, the coals grew much larger and became flaming hot. Angels then took the coals from the altar and flew back to the earth with them in their hands.

I then saw black patches all over the globe. I understood these patches to be specific locations of satan's strongholds on earth. The angels began to throw their "fireballs" into fortifications of darkness, and suddenly demons were scattered, fleeing in terror and screaming in fear. Then I heard the elated explosions of Heaven's laughter. This fiery display reoccurred a number of times with Heaven's demonstrative rejoicing accompanying each victory; and every time Heaven laughed, so did I. The Lord reminded me of Psalm 2:4: *"He who sits in the heavens laughs, the Lord scoffs at them."* My body convulsed with hysterical joy at the very thought of the enemy's defeat. I was witnessing events in the realm of the spirit in the earth from a heavenly and divine perspective.

## Heaven Made an Impact on Me

This heavenly visitation, during a revival meeting in Florida in January 1994, worked many deep things within my heart. First, God began to break my soulish resistance to this new display of His manifest power. My spiritual eyes were also opened, and I realized that there were heavenly parallels that coincided with my natural behavior in the earth. The heavenly encounter was having a profound impact on my life.

As a Kingdom child, I had experienced His power, His glory, and His heart. But these recent revelations were completely new to me and were opening a doorway, a portal, into experiences in glory. In the days that followed, I enjoyed, as well as wrestled, with many supernatural occurrences, including many visions, revelations, angelic visitations, heavenly experiences, power encounters, and supernatural phenomenon that invaded my Christian experience. This, however, was only the beginning. The Lord was preparing my heart to receive increased revelation of heavenly glory. My walk with the Lord was to become more tantalizing, more intimate, and more glorious than I ever could have imagined.

On my return to Canada a few weeks later, I received a call from Mary-Audrey Raycroft, who serves on the pastoral staff of the Toronto Airport Christian Fellowship (TACF), and she described to me how the Holy Spirit had been powerfully released in a fresh outpouring of grace in Canada at TACF. It seemed that masses were experiencing Holy Spirit-inspired laughter and responding in dramatic ways to His supernatural touch. Thousands began to experience spiritual phenomenon that have literally shaken the Church on a global level since that time.

Things would never be the same. An unsatisfied hunger and thirst for His tangible presence now burned inside of God's people, and believers were traveling from all over the world in planes, cars, vans, buses, and trains, to partake of this wonderful and glorious outpouring of the Spirit of God. Why? Because most believers are absolutely desperate to experience the Lord and His supernatural Kingdom in tangible and meaningful ways.

## Off to Toronto

After Mary-Audrey's phone call, I traveled to Toronto for a few days to see what was happening. The encounter I had in Florida was still alive in my spirit, and I hungered for more understanding. But when I arrived in Toronto, I entered into total shock. I saw spontaneous, Spirit-inspired laughter break out all over the meetings in which folks were acting drunk just like the description of the believers in Acts chapter 2 on the day of Pentecost. I was fairly comfortable with the surroundings due to my own experience with the laughter in Florida, but there were other things happening that made no sense to me whatsoever. For example, some individuals were bouncing around like pogo sticks, making strange noises, and flailing around in ways I had never seen before. This all seemed so disruptive, especially when it was occurring during the worship service.

I struggled greatly believing this to be a move of demonic deception. I then made an appointment with John Arnott, pastor and overseer of TACF. He listened very lovingly as I shared my concerns, and then he said some things I will never forget. He encouraged me not to throw away my discernment but also exhorted me to not judge too quickly. He stated that, "Oftentimes we judge things we don't understand." He went on to share with me accounts of historical revivals where similar manifestations broke out in the midst of Sovereign visitations. And he pointed me to some Scriptures and historical writings regarding unique and non-conventional ways that God moved at times in and through His people both in Bible days and throughout church history. He also reminded me that man's tendency is to look to the outward appearance of things but God looks to the heart (see 1 Sam. 16:7). He further encouraged me to interview folks who I saw manifesting in strange ways. He said, "Ask them what the Father is doing in their heart."

And I did exactly that. I found out very quickly that during these strange encounters the Lord was accomplishing things in people's lives in just a few moments that would ordinarily take years of counseling and prayer to obtain. And I discovered great joy and intense, radical, passion for God in these individuals.

If this was "church," it definitely looked different. God was pouring out new wine, and we certainly needed a new wineskin, a new theological grid, to hold what the Lord was granting. At this point, I would like to mention that Stacey Campbell—who is recognized as a prophetic voice to the Body of Christ, and along with her husband, Wesley, are founders of New Life Church in Kelowna, Canada, and Praying The Bible International—prophesied during the '90s outpouring that we would need a container for the times and we couldn't go into the past to find it. She further prophesied that some of the things God was leading us into had never been done before. (See Eyes and Wings Prophecy on Extreme Disciples' CD.)

Over the next number of years, following the initial visitation in 1994, theologians, revival historians, and mature prophets and pastors were raised up to help the Body understand what the Spirit had initiated through this outpouring. This season of visitation opened up a new spiritual era—an era where spiritual sensitivity increased and where heavenly perspective became a revealed position to live from. John Arnott explained to those who couldn't wrap their minds around what was happening that, "sometimes God will offend the mind in order to expose the heart." It is interesting that often the Lord will use offensive packaging in order to find true seekers just as was done in the days of Jesus. Many religious individuals and leaders couldn't embrace Jesus and His ways because He was too controversial, too different, too out-of-the-box, and not at all what they were expecting the Messiah's mode of operation to look like. They needed a new wineskin to hold the new wine. And so do we.

## When in Doubt, Check It Out!

In the Book of Acts, we witness the apostles preaching the Gospel and manifesting the Lord's great power. Signs and wonders confirmed the word they proclaimed, and yet, we find that the new revelation (the Gospel) they carried was offensive to many and triggered great persecution. Like those offended in Acts, we also often reject, or even take offense, at what we do not understand. Scripture, however, gives us an example of a people, the Bereans, who kept their hearts open to the Lord, searching the Scriptures daily to see *"whether those things were so." As a result, they were called "more noble than those in Thessalonica"* (Acts 17:11b KJV).

Notice the Word says that they *"searched the Scriptures daily,* [to see] *whether those things were so"*—they weren't attempting to discover if these things were *not* so. There is a big difference!

*The Word of God must be the standard by which we weigh everything we experience.* It is our plumb line! The Scriptures contain everything we need to understand concerning life and godliness. God's Word is true and must not be compromised. We should, however, be open to seeing things in the Word that we have never noticed before. The Word of God is not simply print on a page; neither is it mere language. No, it is much more than those things. The Word of God is living, eternal, pulsating God-life and needs to be revealed by the Spirit of God. The Word is the full expression and communication of Jesus Himself as both God and Man, and we are to daily pursue the fresh "manna" from Heaven in the revealed Word of God.

The Scriptures reveal the person of God, His laws, and His ways; and every Scripture verse has layers of eternal revelation within it. This year you might get a much fuller revelation than you had of the same Scripture five years ago. It will take eternity to behold the fullness of all that God is, has, and does. He is bigger than we can ever comprehend, and we will never in this life have the full understanding of all that He is. The Holy Spirit, however, has been given to us that we might know the truth and the even the deep things of God. In Deuteronomy 29:29, the Scripture teaches us: *"The secret things belong to the Lord our God, but the things revealed belong to us and to our* [children] *forever, that we may observe all the words of this law."* God reveals the deep things of His Kingdom to those who are hungry and to those who are true seekers. *"For to us God revealed them through the Spirit; for the Spirit searches all things, even the depths of God"* (1 Cor. 2:10).

A revelation of truth will not just be found in one Scripture portion. Once you receive a revelation or insight from the Spirit of God, you will be able to compare it to other Scriptures and find other portions that bear witness to that principle or revelation. You will also discover that the nature and character of God will support your revelation as well as the things the Lord has performed in previous moves of the Spirit. All these things will bring confirmation to your revelation. In supernatural encounters, you will never find the Lord performing things that are contrary to His Word or His character. You always need to verify that the Word supports your heavenly or supernatural experiences.

Furthermore, you cannot assume that revelation of the Word given to the Body of Christ in previous seasons is complete enough to embrace what the Lord is currently doing. Prior to the Protestant Reformation, there were common Christian beliefs that were confronted through the new revelation Luther received from the Lord. *"The righteous lives by his faith"* (Rom. 1:17b) hit organized religion like a bomb and confronted the legalistic and clergy/laity mentality that was prevalent in that time. Subsequently, a theological war was launched and Luther's reputation and life were in danger. Looking back now, we all can breathe a sigh of relief that the revelation of the righteous being saved by faith was contended for. Although the institutionalized church of that era couldn't see it or agree with it, it was of God nonetheless. God was giving a new wineskin to hold the new wine of the reformation and to challenge some of the deception and error of the previous state of the church.

New things are difficult for most to absorb. Many in the church are uncomfortable with change, but it is so necessary when God is moving forward. If Israel had refused to follow the cloud as God led them through the wilderness, they would have died in the desert. Likewise, perhaps many Christians are walking in a dry and thirsty land because they have not discerned the changing of the seasons.

In Matthew chapter 9, we find Jesus being confronted by the Pharisees because He was eating with tax collectors and sinners. They believed that in order to be holy, one must refuse to associate with others who could defile them. This was their interpretation of the Scriptures and their law. Although there is some truth within this mind-set, it is not the full revelation of the heart of God. Jesus answered by pointing them to the Scripture. In verse 13, we find Him instructing them to *"go and learn what this means: 'I desire compassion, and not sacrifice,' for I did not come to call the righteous, but sinners"* (Matt. 9:13).

That made no sense to them whatsoever. They were locked in to what they understood the Scriptures to teach and were not open to further revelation. In fact, the Scripture that Jesus quoted them did not even specifically give endorsement to what He was doing. He was calling them to pray and seek for understanding from God concerning His heart. If they would have been opened to discovering the truth, they would have searched the Scripture and prayed for the Lord to open their eyes, and He would have! They should have been like the faithful Bereans and searched the Scriptures to see if the things Jesus was saying were so.

Later, when the disciples came to Jesus privately, He explained to them a powerful truth: *"Nor do people put new wine into old wineskins; otherwise the wineskins burst, and the wine pours out and the wineskins are ruined; but they put new wine into fresh wineskins, and both are preserved"* (Matt. 9:17).

The old, religious, theological grid of the past cannot hold what the Lord does in the next move. Each move needs a new spiritual perspective of what God is doing, and this perspective must be initiated by fresh revelation, not human ingenuity. As in every move of God, it is possible that past revelation can create inflexible mind-sets that seek to control what God wants to do. And if we are not careful, we can allow past revelation to become hardened tradition that will endanger the next move of God. In Mark 7:9, Jesus told the religious folk of His day that *"You are experts at setting aside the commandment of God in order to keep your tradition."*

In this hour of spiritual revolution, we must seek the Lord for a new wineskin. We need to be diligent to search out the Scriptures, inviting the Holy Spirit to reveal light and truth. Let's fervently follow Him as He leads and guides us into revolution.

*Things which eye has not seen and ear has not heard, and which have not entered the heart of man, all that God has prepared for those who love Him. For to us God revealed them through the Spirit; for the Spirit searches all things, even the depths of God (1 Corinthians 2:9-10).*

Chapter Four

# Spirit Man Arise

Picking up the phone, I heard the voice of the daughter of my friend and coworker, Donna Bromley. Her tone was urgent as she requested emergency prayer for her mother who had just been admitted to the hospital. Donna's situation seemed grave—the medical staff suspected a pulmonary embolism. Understanding the seriousness of such a life-threatening condition, I was immediately overcome with a prayer burden. Linda Palone, a friend who happened to be visiting at the time, joined me in intercession as we quickly put on our coats and charged out the door for a prayer walk, determined to wrestle this through to victory!

At the time, I was living in Mesa, Arizona, and this power walk took us down the main street of the city with four lanes of noisy traffic whizzing by. I must say that we were storming Heaven in an exceedingly loud fashion (praying aggressively—some tongues and some in English—the fervent, effectual prayer) as we violently claimed the Lord's promise of victory for Donna. One of the Scriptures that came to me during our prayer time was

Ephesians 1:3: *"Blessed be the God and Father of our Lord Jesus Christ, who has blessed us with every spiritual blessing in the heavenly places in Christ."*

## Inside Ephesians 1:3

Despite the heavy prayer burden that I was experiencing, I found that a deep peace was settling in upon me as I meditated on and confessed this particular portion of Scripture I found that a deep peace was settling in upon me. I began to experience a sense of rich spiritual pleasantness in my soul and felt the Lord's presence strong around me. In the very next moment, however, I sensed that I had entered into the depths of spiritual reality that is expressed in Ephesians 1:3. I was in what is called a trance vision. In this type of vision, you are in a dream-like state yet remain awake and are oftentimes aware of your natural surroundings. In other words, you are "inside" the vision.

Again, from James Goll's book, *The Seer*, he offers some valuable insight into the spiritual experience of a trance.

> *Ekstasis* also means "trance," as in Acts 10:10 when Peter has his vision on the rooftop in Joppa before his visit to Cornelius: "But he became hungry and was desiring to eat; but while they were making preparations, he fell into a trance [ekstasis]." A similar thing happened to Paul one day when he was praying at the temple in Jerusalem: "And it happened when I returned to Jerusalem and was praying in the temple, that I fell into a trance [ekstasis], and I saw Him saying to me, 'Make haste, and get out of Jerusalem quickly, because they will not accept your testimony about Me'" (Acts 22:17-18).

A trance is a form of ecstatic experience. In our day and age, trances have gotten a bad name because of their association with the New Age movement and the occult. The experiences of Peter and Paul reveal that a trance, although perhaps not as common as some other types of visions, is nonetheless a legitimate and biblical form of visionary state that God may choose to use in imparting revelation to His people.[1]

While I was in my Ephesians 1:3 spiritual trance-like experience, I stood on the sidewalk beside the public thoroughfare, hearing all the traffic sounds, and was completely aware of my environment. In fact, I even remember saying to Linda, who was walking beside me, "Oh my goodness, I am in Ephesians 1:3!" Please understand that my body, mind, will, and emotions were all intact and very aware of everything around me. In my body, I was on the main street in Mesa, Arizona; however, in my spirit, I sensed that I was inside the tangible, eternal dimension of the rich realties that Paul was writing about in Ephesians. I sensed that I was there in those heavenly places in Christ.

Jesus said in John 6:63b, *"The words that I have spoken to you are spirit and are life."* The written Word that we read in the Scriptures represents the actual substance of what is being communicated. The revelation within the Scriptures is a living, eternal substance. When we come to understand this, we will begin to move out of an academic understanding of the Scripture into spiritual revelation. There is a dimension in God that will enable us to go beyond the mere reading of the Scriptures. The Scriptures are not like any other book. It is not that they are magical; rather they have a spiritual dimension to them. When our eyes are open, we are able to enter into and experience the Incarnate Word, Christ Himself. To be inside the Word is to be inside Christ, who is the Word, the Logos of God.

If we make it our practice to simply seek intellectual understanding of this Book, then we will never have our eyes opened. However, those who approach its words with spiritual hunger and vibrant faith are the ones whose eyes will be open to see spiritual truth and enter into its spiritual realities. To these little ones, the Father will show the Son of His love, who is on every page of the Holy Scriptures. He will draw you into that word so that you can experience the Word.

While in this Ephesians 1:3 encounter, I was very aware of the reality of the place where I found myself. It was a spiritual place and in it were spiritual blessings of every kind. I sensed that I was experiencing the blessings of wisdom, grace, love, joy, reconciliation, prosperity, health, strength, and favor. In this experience, the Lord did give me an acute ability to discern which blessings were which. When you are in the realm of the spirit, you just know things although you have never been taught those things through natural training. I knew at that moment the rich reality of those spiritual blessings. They were no longer mere words but had become for me a spiritual reality that would impact my life forever.

The Holy Spirit's presence was very real to me at the time. I was aware that as a covenant child, legal access to all these blessings had been given to me. I also had the sense that I was to wait on the Holy Spirit to show me how to move through this experience and not grasp for control. While in this realm, a strong desire to respect, honor, and submit to His leading rose within me. The communication between the Holy Spirit and me was Spirit-to-spirit, and no audible words were spoken. I knew what He was thinking and was aware that He knew my thoughts as well.

## Depositing the Healing Blessing

During the encounter, the Holy Spirit led me to take hold of the healing blessing He revealed to me. I did so. How? The best way to explain this encounter is to describe it as a "faith connection." I knew by faith and a deep inner assurance, an intense knowing, that I was handling the unseen substance of healing. The Bible teaches us that faith is the evidence of things unseen (see Heb. 11:1). When you are in God's kind of faith, you know, that you know, that you know. (We will discuss more about faith in another chapter.) During Holy Spirit-directed spiritual encounters, you respond when He speaks because you believe Him. At the moment the faith agreement and cooperation with the Holy Spirit takes place, supernatural encounters can occur.

As I continued to experience the trance-like vision, the Holy Spirit led me to minister the healing blessing to my friend, Donna. In the natural, she was about 1,500 miles away in a hospital bed in Vancouver, Canada, and I was in Mesa, Arizona. How, then, was I to minister the healing blessing to my friend? All I can say is that the very moment I came into faith agreement with the Spirit's leading, I found myself within the vision, hovering over Donna in a hospital bed. I saw her as clear as I would see something in the natural realm. By faith, I released the healing blessing to her and then was immediately out of the encounter with an absolute confidence that she was healed. I had full assurance that she was going to be all right! Later on that evening, I received a phone call from her daughter saying that following some further observations, the doctors believed that if she remained stable throughout the night they would send her home in the morning.

The Bible shares some examples that might highlight the validity of such experiences where a believer is somewhere in the spirit that is different from the location of their natural body. One example is Elisha. We know that Elisha was a very spiritually sensitive man and seemingly saw in the unseen dimension on a regular basis. In Second Kings 6:8-14 we read the story of the king of Aram who was strategizing to conquer Israel. Each time that the king of Aram planned to attack Israel, Elisha would warn the king of Israel of the king of Aram's specific battle strategy so that Israel could guard themselves. After this happened on a number of occasions, the king of Aram became enraged and thought there was a traitor in his camp, revealing his battle plans. In verse 12, his servant states, *"No, my lord, O king; but Elisha, the prophet who is in Israel, tells the king of Israel the words that you speak in your bedroom."* Elisha was obviously never found to be physically in the natural realm of the king of Aram's bedchamber, but perhaps he was there in the spirit or in a vision.

In John 1:47-51, we find Nathanael absolutely amazed that Jesus saw him under the fig tree *before* Philip called him. It could be a possibility that Jesus was actually with him in the spirit. Whatever the case, Jesus assured Nathanael that he would see even more things than that: *"...thou shalt see greater things than these....Hereafter ye shall see heaven open, and the angels of God ascending and descending upon the Son of Man"* (John 1:50-51 KJV).

In First Corinthians 5:3, Paul states, *"For I, on my part, though absent in body but present in spirit, have already judged him who has so committed this, as though I were present."* I realize that we use the terminology, "I will be with you in spirit" to communicate that our heart will be connected to those we are not with in body. It is interesting, however, to read through this passage in First Corinthians 5. In verse 4 Paul goes on to say, *"In the name of our Lord Jesus, **when you are assembled, and I with you in spirit**, with the power of our Lord Jesus"* (emphasis added). We do know that transport in the spirit is possible when under the complete direction of the Holy Spirit.

Now, you might be asking, "Did your spirit leave your body when you went to Vancouver in the visionary encounter? Was this an out-of-the-body experience?" Let me try to explain to you what I believe concerning these types of phenomena. First of all, I do not believe that a person's spirit ever fully leaves their body unless they have expired. The spirit in you is your breath, your life. When your spirit leaves, your life leaves, and there is nothing left to sustain your physical body. As a nurse in a cardiovascular ward, I was at the bedside of many folks when they took their last breath. When their spirit departed, they no longer had life or breath in their physical bodies after that moment. Sometimes when we had successfully resuscitated an individual, he or she would attempt to describe to us how they felt their inner selves leave their bodies. They even at times described us resuscitating them. In these cases, they were actually raised from the dead. The life in them had left, and their physical bodies ceased to function. Their cardiac monitor confirmed the flat-line activity of the heart and their respirations had ceased. Through cardiac massage, however, their life returned. This is another topic altogether, but even as some healings take place through medical treatment and surgical procedures and others through miracles, we acknowledge that Christ Himself is the source of these healings irregardless of how the healing is ministered. The same is with the raising of the dead. Sometimes it is through natural means and other times through supernatural means, but the Source of life is the same in both—Christ Himself.

In Second Corinthians 12:2, Paul stated as he was explaining a Third Heaven experience, *"whether in the body or out of the body I cannot tell."* In other words, this experience was so alive and real to him that he wasn't sure if he was "out of the body" (expired), or if he was in his spirit. He couldn't tell, but he concluded, "God knows."

As a born-again believer, your spirit man has been made alive in Christ. If you are "in the spirit" during a God-encounter, even though it might seem that your spirit has left your body, it has actually not. Your spirit man simply has the ability to function beyond the limitations of your physical body when under the influence and inspiration of the Holy Spirit.

The human mind can also function beyond the body's limitation. I can be washing dishes with my physical body but my thoughts might be beyond my body and beyond the sink full of dishes. I could be daydreaming in my thoughts, perhaps as far as the beaches of Hawaii.

Even as our thoughts can think beyond the body while the mind remains within the body so can our spirit function beyond the body and yet still be within.

## No Time or Distance in the Spirit

In the spiritual dimension there is no time or distance. As we began to point out, when you are in the spirit, it is possible to be in one place one moment and in the next moment somewhere else when the Spirit chooses. When walking in the spirit, you will not be confined to the limitations of the natural realm. Ezekiel the prophet experienced this type of spiritual phenomenon when, as recounted in Ezekiel chapter 8, he was taken by the Lord into the innermost part of the temple to see the corruption. In the spiritual dimension, it is possible to experience timeless encounters. One moment, you might be aware of your natural surroundings and in the very next moment, you could be like Ezekiel who was brought into a different location from his natural domain in order to see things through God's understanding. Oftentimes, experiences in the unseen, timeless, dimensions are only a thought away.

John the Beloved, while on the Isle of Patmos, experienced an immediate "experience in the glory realm" as we read of his heavenly encounters in the Book of Revelation chapters 4 and 5.

The Scripture also gives examples of individuals such as Philip who experienced a spiritual translation where his entire body, soul, and spirit were transported to another revival after he led the Ethiopian eunuch to the Lord (see Acts 8:36-40).

It appears that Jesus, following His resurrection, possibly walked through the wall into the midst of the locked room where His disciples were meeting. He was there, not only in His spirit but in His body as well. It was at that time He told Thomas to touch His hands and His side as proof that it was really Him (see John 20:26-27). Many believers are experiencing transport in the spirit in the ways described in these Bible examples. Jesus said that the works He did we will do also (see John 14:12).

When you are in the spirit, it is possible to see through God's empowerment into the past, present, and future as the Holy Spirit directs. Daniel, for instance, saw into the future when he prophetically viewed the end-time visions in the Book of Daniel. So also did John as he scribed the visions we see written in the Book of Revelation. I believe Moses saw into the past when he wrote the Book of Genesis. He was possibly shown those details by God when the Lord revealed the "*back parts*" of His glory in Exodus 33:23.

There are a few sensitive believers in Christ who have spiritual encounters that are not limited by time or distance. However, as in all things, we must be willing to test the spirit. Because of the potential for deception and because we are imperfect vessels we must be willing to submit our experiences to the Scriptures and to those in leadership.

## In the Spirit yet Aware of the Natural

During the entire Ephesians 1:3 spiritual encounter and while symbolically depositing the healing blessing, I was aware of my natural surroundings. I even continued talking to Linda during this time. I said, "You'll never believe this: In the spirit, I went to Vancouver and gave Donna a healing blessing and she is healed!" I *knew* it! I had never had such confidence before. I knew I was under the Holy Spirit's direction, leading, and power the entire time. My spirit was not removed from my body, but I was experiencing something in my spirit that my body was not engaged in. This spiritual activity was beyond the body, yet my spirit was still in the body. I want to stress again, that this was all done under the unction and direction of the Holy Spirit.

In New Age cults, many are trained in the spiritual exercise of astral travel as we mentioned earlier. The difference in these New Age practices, however, is most of the time, without realizing it, the practitioner actually gives himself over to a demonic entity. Spiritual activity such as this, when it is outside of the direction of the Holy Spirit, is absolutely forbidden in Scripture.

> *When thou art come into the land which the Lord thy God giveth thee, thou shalt not learn to do after the abominations of those nations. There shall not be found among you any one that maketh his son or his daughter to pass through the fire, or that useth divination, or an observer of times, or an enchanter, or a witch, or a charmer, or a consulter with familiar spirits, or a wizard, or a necromancer. For all that do these things are an abomination unto the Lord: and*

*because of these abominations the Lord thy God doth drive*
*them out from before thee. Thou shalt be perfect with the*
*Lord thy God* (Deuteronomy 18:9-13 KJV).

## Source Is Everything
## in These Types of Spiritual Encounters!

I remained in the Ephesians 1:3 experience for about 40 minutes that evening. My sensitivity to the supernatural realm had
waned a bit following my visionary activity in Vancouver, but I still
enjoyed fresh revelation of the Word of God and a strong sense of
the Lord's presence as we completed our walk. The next day, I
received the report that Donna had been discharged in good
health. Praise the Lord! It is always nice to receive confirmations,
but in this particular situation, I knew that I knew that I knew she
was healed! *"Blessed be the God and Father of our Lord Jesus*
*Christ, who has blessed us with every spiritual blessing in the heav-*
*enly places in Christ"* (Eph. 1:3).

## Ministry in China

One time I met a group of intercessors who had an amazing
God-encounter during a prayer meeting in the community of
Mount Ephraim, New Jersey. The prayer leader explained to me
that they had been meeting every week for about a year. She continued to testify that one particular day during their scheduled
meeting, they all were led unexpectedly by the Spirit into a prison
in China. Their natural bodies were in the U.S.A. but in the spirit, they were in China. They found themselves in a prison cell with
a Christian man who had been imprisoned for his faith. They all
saw each other there. They ministered to him and then all came

out of the vision at the same time. The leader of the prayer meeting instructed them not to say anything concerning what they had just experienced but to write it out first. She then had each of them read their reports, of which they all matched. They had not gone into prayer that day expecting this to happen; however, the Holy Spirit led. We have heard of many similar testimonies.

I believe that the spiritual encounters that I have just described will excite and motivate many to pursue deeper intimacy with the Lord and to search for truth. For others, my stories could possibly stir skepticism, confusion, or even fear, especially if "new creation realities" are not fully understood. In Second Corinthians 5:17 we read, *"Therefore if anyone is in Christ, he is a new creature; the old things passed away; behold, new things have come."*

## Spirit, Soul, and Body

We acknowledge according to Scripture that we are a three-part being consisting of a spirit, soul, and body (see 1 Thess. 5:23). The creation account confirms this fact. In Genesis 2:7, the Scripture says, *"Then the Lord God formed man of dust from the ground, and breathed into his nostrils the breath of life; and man became a living being* [soul].*"*

We see in this passage that man was "formed" of the dust of the ground referring to man's physical makeup, his body. Next, the Lord then breathed "the breath of life" into man. This breath of God became man's spirit; that is the principle life within him. It was God's breath that created man's spirit or life. As soon as the breath of God entered the formed dust, a soul was produced.

The spirit of man relates to the spirit realm and is where our God-consciousness dwells. It occupies the innermost part of our being and is sensitive and able to interact with the spirit world and with God. God is spirit and those who interact with Him through prayer, worship, and communion do so in that realm of the spirit and according to truth. Unfortunately, rationalism has in many cases stolen from us the joy and wonder of spiritual Christianity.

The soul of man consists of our mind, will, imagination, and emotions and is self-conscious. It is the seat of our personality. The soul is in touch with both the relational and the rational realms. Intellect, thought, emotions, choice, decision, and vision are all experiences of the soul. These faculties are what are engaged in the building of relationship both with God and man.

The body of man, being formed of physical substance, relates to the physical realm and is more world conscious. It carries out the choices of the soul and is a container for the soul and spirit. The body does the work through the physical senses and organs.

When a person is born again, it is the spirit that is actually born again. Jesus said in John 3:6, *"That which is born of the flesh is flesh, and that which is born of the Spirit is spirit."* At the point of being born again, Christ's Spirit enters a person's human spirit, and he experiences new birth. At that point, the person is a new creation and old things are passed away; all things have become new.

I clearly remember when I received Christ into my heart. I was completely convinced that I was different inside and yet all things had not become new. Even though I felt accepted, clean within, full of hope, and overjoyed at the thought of having my sins forgiven, I still had the same physical form and shape that I had before I prayed. My physical body hadn't changed one single bit (even though I would have welcomed some change indeed). My soul wasn't completely made new, either, for I soon discovered that some of my thoughts, attitudes, and reactions seemed to betray the Christ-like nature that I had been filled with.

You see, it is not our body or soul that is born again. It is our spirit. Our spirit man comes alive with the very nature and character of Jesus Christ at the time of our rebirth. We are filled with His righteousness and His glory, and are given everything that pertains to life and to godliness (see 2 Pet. 1:3). We are absolutely perfect and complete within our born-again spirit nature.

Salvation is a gift, and all Christ's glory and perfection are given to us by His grace. Your old spiritual nature cannot be found after you are born again. It is like pouring yourself a cup of clear tea. After you have added cream, you can neither separate the tea from the cream nor the cream from the tea. You now have a brand-new drink. The old is gone. When you receive the Spirit of Christ into your life, your spirit man becomes a brand-new life. No longer can you separate yourself from Him or Him from you.

We are called to live by our spirit that is in harmony with God's Spirit so that we will not fulfill the desire of the flesh. The spirit man, under the direction of the Holy Spirit, will eventually bring renewal to the soul if the soul follows the leading and unction of the born-again spirit. The soul is not to prevail over the spirit, but rather to submit to it. The human will constantly makes choices of whether to follow the spirit or the dictates of the soul as manifested in the lusts of the flesh, the lust of the eyes, and the pride of life. The body then carries out that choice. We live in the reality of what Paul expressed in chapter 12 of his letter to the Romans. *"I beseech you therefore, brethren, by the mercies of God, that ye present your bodies a living sacrifice, holy, acceptable unto God, which is your reasonable service. And be not conformed to this world: but be ye transformed by the renewing of your mind, that ye may prove what is that good, and acceptable, and perfect, will of God"* (Rom. 12:1-2 KJV).

Let me further illustrate the principle of living by the leading of our born-again spirit.

## I Was Spiritually Dull and Empty

In December 2000, I was in the midst of a prayer retreat as is my custom every year. I was enjoying a month of personal devotion as well as a concentrated time of seeking the Lord for the word that He wanted me to carry in the next year as an itinerant prophetic minister. At this particular year's prayer retreat, I was feeling very dull and spiritually empty, even though I was diligently positioning myself for hours each day in prayer, study, and seeking the Lord's face.

Toward the end of the month I was feeling a little panic, for I had not yet received a clear word from the Lord for the new year. After I had pressed in for some answers, the Lord made it clear to me that He was going to lead me into a season in which I would not actually experience His manifest presence, His glory, or His love very much at all. He further revealed that I wouldn't even sense my own personal love or passion for Him. I would feel empty and lifeless and void of emotion.

"Why?" I asked. (I actually didn't think this was a brilliant idea at all.)

"Because I am going to teach you how to live out of your spirit this year," He replied in that proverbial, still, small voice. "I am going to show you how to strengthen your spirit, and in order to do so, I am removing your ability to lean on your soul or flesh."

He gave me two keys at that time to strengthen my spirit man. The first was to pray with violent and aggressive faith, praying in tongues every day. The second was to daily confess the covenant promises of the Word of God over my life. I soon realized that when you are void of emotion, there is no motivation at all to exert any kind of heartfelt energy, let alone violence. The exercise was good for me, though, because it forced me to live out of obedience to what the Lord had spoken to my spirit and not out of how I felt within my soul or body.

It was an interesting year. Many of my close friends were experiencing numerous manifestations of the glory of the Lord on a daily basis. My personal intercessor phoned late one afternoon, absolutely thrilled to tell me about the visitation of the Lord's glory in her home prayer meeting earlier that day. She described in detail how each intercessor was deeply touched for hours by the glory that had manifested in the meeting.

No sooner had I completed that phone call than another friend and coworker came by to visit, and believe me, she was a "shiner." She had a "glory glow" all over her and began to describe the wonderful downloads she was experiencing while in a deep, intimate place of heart connection with the Lord that morning.

As for me, I was feeling dull, unaware of any strong sense of elation, and definitely not experiencing a "glory glow." Have you ever personally experienced times when you felt like you were the wart on the Body of Christ? You know what I mean—everyone is getting touched, blasted, visited, glorified. As for you? Nothing...empty...dry. It certainly does give you a tremendous opportunity to fight off rejection, isolation, and fear of abandonment. Anyway, as I was choosing to "rejoice with those who rejoice," a thought came to me: *I am just as much in the glory, in His presence, and in His power as they are. It's just that my soul and body aren't feeling it right now. It is all taking place in my spirit.* Now, that was a God-thought for sure!

This was not just a thought process I came up with in order to justify or validate my position as a cherished child of God. This was real, raw truth, and I came undone at the very thought of it. We are as complete as we are going to be in Christ. He is in us. He is the King of glory. He is the hope of glory. He is glory, and all His promises to us as covenant children of God are yes and amen!

On the cross, He has already secured for us every spiritual blessing in the heavenly places. He has given all things for us to enjoy. We don't have to continue to hope and pray that we can get close to Him, feel Him, or receive one of His manifold blessings. He has already completed the work on the cross to give us access to everything in the Kingdom. This is so glorious. This is truth!

## In the Glory Realm

The Lord is calling us all to live out of our spirits. In our spirits, we cannot get any closer to Him than we are right now. Our spirits are vitally and eternally one with the Lord and with His entire Kingdom. As we become acquainted with our spirit man, we will sense more of what is available to us in the glory realm, the spiritual realm.

It is the Word of God that rightly divides between the soul and spirit (see Heb. 4:12). Our born-again spirit will always adhere to the truth of the Word of God regardless of our thoughts, feelings, or circumstances. As we become more familiar with the operation of our spirit man, we will become more sensitive to God's Word, His will, and His ways. We will begin to experience and discern the supernatural as we become increasingly aware of our spiritual nature. Our emotions will be up and down at times. They can betray us. Our thoughts can deceive us. However, our born-again spirits are bound to, and are filled with, His presence and His truth at all times.

The Lord had me journey through this "season of walking out of my spirit" by faith for almost an entire year. Every once in a while, I would get a little reprieve, but for the most part, I was very aware of dryness and lived in a sense of feeling extremely empty. In the midst of this, though, the truth in my spirit rose up strong and embraced new creation realities. I didn't live out of my emotions; I was very numb emotionally. I didn't live out of my reasonings; they were confused. And I experienced horrific levels of warfare to a point where every area of my life and ministry seemed to be challenged in deep and painful ways. Yet my spirit remained strong. I always had the truth to lean on. I could live out of the safety and security of my spirit, where I held on to victory through it all. The daily decrees of the promises of God over my life and the hour each day I prayed in tongues truly gave definition to my spirit.

I literally had to choose with an act of my will to engage in my daily discipline of prayer and confessions of the Word. Did I feel inspired to pray? Absolutely not. Did I feel anointed to decree the truth of the Word of God. No way. The carnal mind is at odds against the Spirit.

> Because the carnal mind is **enmity** against God: for it is not subject to the law of God, neither indeed can be (Romans 8:7 KJV, emphasis added).

When you don't feel motivated or inspired, it is difficult to stir up a good scriptural confession of any kind. Your mind is blank, your passion is nonexistent. Even though I did not feel inspired, I still chose to obey. I searched the Bible and looked for verses that proclaimed who I was and I wrote them down. Every day I disciplined myself to read those confessions for at least an hour. Those confessions are now written in a little booklet called *Decree*, but back then, it was pages of foolscap. I had to win a struggle against my flesh. I believed the instruction of the Lord. It was faith that produced obedience. The disciplines I learned back then have since been woven into my life and ministry, and have given me strength to stand in difficult situations with a deep sense of peace, covering, and inner assurance. I truly learned what it meant to "walk by faith and not by sight."

By the end of the season, I had learned to love this walk of faith. It is not that I don't enjoy spiritual experience in the realm of emotions and outward circumstances. I definitely do. I am absolutely convinced that the Lord desires His children to enjoy experiential activity with Him daily; that is why I have written this book. More precious to me, though, is that His truth abides forever and will remain steadfast and immovable within our spirits, even if everything else in and around us is dull, dead, or shaky. In these cases, the walk of faith as you stand on the truth of who you are in Christ actually becomes your experience. We can be completely confident in our relationship with God as we seek Him for experience, whether we are touched in tangible ways or not. We have been truly blessed and filled with His greatness and glory. The Kingdom realm is home for us.

All that Christ is, we are in Him. All that Christ has, we have in Him. An invitation has been set before us as His dear and precious covenant children to explore the fullness of His presence. Let us then enter into the reality of the substance of the Word of God. Let us imbibe of all His blessings and experience His goodness, for we truly are a new creature in Christ Jesus; *"the old things passed away; behold, new things have come"* (2 Cor. 5:17b).

# Endnote

1. Jim W. Goll, *The Seer* (Shippensburg, PA: Destiny Image Publishers, 2004).

Chapter Five

---

# THE VITAL CONNECTOR

In the previous chapter, we discovered that all Christ is, and all He has, belongs to us through Him in our born-again spiritual nature. We learned that faith in who God says we are as a born-again child of God shapes and forms our lives. Absolutely everything that pertains to life and to godliness has already been given to us through Christ's redemptive work on the cross. That includes forgiveness, mercy, provision, health and healing, strength, the presence of the Lord, angelic visitation, His fire, His glory, spiritual vision, fellowship with the Holy Spirit, and everything we need to live a fulfilled and victorious life in the Kingdom of God.

The question for many is: how do we secure the blessings from the heavenly places into our everyday life here on the earth? The answer is simple—by faith. Faith is the connector that secures all the covenant blessings, wrought through Christ's finished work on the cross, into our everyday lives.

## A Little Connector Called Faith

It is extremely important, then, that we understand how to release our faith in order to experience the realms of heavenly glory. How do we get saved? By faith. How do we access the throne of grace? By faith. How do we engage in communion with God? By faith. How do we enter the glory cloud? By faith. How do we see angels? By faith. How do we sense His presence? By faith. There is nothing too mystical about spiritual experience. It is all based on the infallibility of the Word of God and is accessed through a little connector called faith.

Faith is the foundational force that launches us into all Kingdom experience. Hebrews 11:6 says that, *"without faith it is impossible to please Him, for he who comes to God must believe that He is and that He is a rewarder of those who seek Him."*

Hebrews 11:1 declares that *"faith is the substance of things hoped for, the evidence of things not seen"* (KJV). In other words, faith is the connector or the "downloader," so to speak, of heavenly blessings. Throughout this chapter, we will attempt to dissect faith. I remember loving biology in school, especially when we had the opportunity to take little animals apart and examine all their intricate organs, discovering how every part functioned. Welcome, then, to Faith 101. Put on your lab coats as we enter the faith observation laboratory.

Over 20 years ago at a conference in Vancouver, Canada, I heard Jerry Savelle, a popular Christian preacher, share a sermon on faith. I have never forgotten that message and over the years I have meditated on it, acted on it, and developed the principles into a teaching that has now since been shared all over the world. Following is a brief overview of that teaching.

# Faith Hears

Romans 10:17 tells us, *"So faith comes from hearing, and hearing by the word* [rhema] *of Christ."* Faith comes through a posture of hearing and listening. The word "rhema" in this passage generally refers to the quickened word that the Holy Spirit brings to our heart. The *rhema* is a quickened word for a specific situation and is brought to us through the inspiration of the Holy Spirit. It might involve the inspiration of an actual Scripture (*logos*—generally speaking; although there are other uses of the word *logos*), or it could be a word of knowledge, a prophetic word, a still small voice, but it will always be that which produces faith for the victory or provision of Christ in a particular situation.

## *Our Son Was in Trouble*

While in his early teens, one of our sons stepped into some trouble. In discovering the details, we sat him down to talk him through it, and though he was very polite and agreeable throughout the discussion, we were unable to thwart the escapades. He continued on with the activities that concerned us, some of which were life-threatening and illegal. I was a seasoned prayer warrior at the time, and in fact, I had taught seminars on prayer and led intercession meetings for years. During this season, I applied all I knew in the area of prayer, and yet everything seemed to get worse. In the midst of it, I assumed a position of absolute panic and terror most days. I would pray with intense emotion but seem to never hit a breakthrough.

Anxiety was filling my life, thoughts, and emotions; and I was growing very weary in the battle. It is extremely difficult to know that your children are involved in dangerous activities, when you love them so much and want them safe and secure and hidden in the love and righteousness of the Lord. Anxiety, fear, and panic, all symptoms of unbelief that resist the function of faith, were actually working against me as these things provided a landing strip for the enemy.

Eventually, everything concerning my son's activities became exponentially more difficult. Finally, one night, as I wailed out with great intensity, a Scripture was powerfully quickened to me from Isaiah 59:21. I looked it up and read it with anticipation: *"'As for Me, this is My covenant with them', says the Lord: 'My Spirit which is upon you, and My words which I have put in your mouth shall not depart from your mouth, nor from the mouth of your offspring, nor from the mouth of your offspring's offspring,' says the Lord, 'from now and forever.'"*

Oh my goodness, I thought I was going to explode! The promise was so alive, so real! Faith entered my heart at that very moment. It was unshakable. As a result of that quickening, I had complete and total confidence that my son would be protected and rescued. Subsequently, all fear and panic fled in the presence of faith. I knew and believed, without a shadow of a doubt, that he would live secure in the blessings and mercy of God. I remember leaping up out of my chair at that very moment and speaking right into the face of the enemy: "You cannot have my son, for he is a covenant child. You will be sorry you ever tried!"

In the weeks that followed, our son's situation did not noticeably improve, but my reactions certainly changed! Even though the promise hadn't manifested yet, I knew it was a done deal.

Why? Because faith hears. I had heard the voice of victory, and I securely possessed the promise of God that insured the blessing. The victory finally unfolded in the months to follow, and our son was fully restored. The battle, however, was won in prayer that night when faith entered via the "sword of the Spirit." As the

Scripture says, *"This is the victory that has overcome the world—our faith"* (1 John 5:4b).

Our son's breakthrough came when I found one of God's covenant blessings and then called it down from Heaven to earth. It was faith that drew the reality of that promise into my struggle in the earthly realm and secured the heavenly substance of victory. In any of our life situations, faith can hear what the Spirit says to the Church and to our hearts!

In order to *hear* the Word that produces faith, we need to posture ourselves in His presence. The story of Mary and Martha is a perfect example of a posture that anticipates and welcomes *hearing* from the Lord. We find that Mary took that position when she sat at Jesus' feet while Martha was distracted by her many preparations. It is important for us to take time out of the busyness of our day to sit at His feet and listen to what He wants to say to us.

Like the Old Testament prophet Habakkuk, we must also open our spiritual ears and position ourselves to hear from the Lord: *"I will stand on my guard post and station myself on the rampart; and I will keep watch to see what He will speak to me"* (Hab. 2:1).

As we posture ourselves for the Spirit's leading in Kingdom encounters, it is vital that we hear His Word to our hearts. This is what will produce faith to enter into Kingdom experience and victory.

## Faith Sees

Faith always sees through God's eyes and from His perspective. In Genesis 13:14-15, we find God giving Abraham a faith vision. In this Scripture, God speaks with Abraham after he separates from Lot: *"Now lift up your eyes and look from the place where you are, northward and southward and eastward and westward; for all the land which you see, I will give it to you and to your descendants forever."* In other words, He was saying, "If you see it, Abraham, you can have it."

Many times our vision is too small or is distorted, and so we fail and falter along the way. People often "see" themselves through a lying lens and thus believe they are failures, rejects, or worthless. Unfortunately, if that is how they truly see themselves, that is what they will become. As a man thinks in his heart, so is he (see Prov. 23:7a).

Let us look at an example of how our mind-sets influence our lives. The Scripture says that we are *"the righteousness of God in Him* [Christ]*"* (2 Cor. 5:21). Do you believe this? Do you see yourself in right standing with God, or do you see yourself always missing the mark and forever struggling with sin and failure? If you view things from a negative vantage point, you will become what you believe or what you "see." If you see yourself as a sinner, you will sin. If you see yourself as righteous, you will live in righteousness. If the Word says you are righteous, you are righteous. Begin to believe what is true, and feed the vision of that truth into your heart. What you see or perceive is what you will do and be.

### Fact Versus Truth

There is a big difference between *fact* and *truth*. It might be a fact that you committed a sinful act today. You don't need to deny that if you have. You are free to acknowledge that, but remember it is only a fact. Facts are temporal whereas truth is eternal. Truth always usurps fact. What is the truth in this particular scenario? *"If we confess our sins, He is faithful and righteous to forgive us our sins and to cleanse us from all unrighteousness"* (1 John 1:9).

Finished. No guilt, no shame. You might say, "But I don't feel cleansed or forgiven." In the faith realm, feelings are not valid if they are contrary to the truth. You are absolutely and completely righteous in Christ. This is the truth whether you feel it or not, and truth prevails over the fact. Your actions and behavior will eventually come into line with what you truly believe.

Now, let's apply this principle to the realm of spiritual experience. Do you believe that you are a person who can experience the glory presence of God? Do you see yourself as a spiritually sensitive child of God? Do you believe that through the eye of faith you can see the reality of the truth concerning the throne room, the angels, and the glory cloud of the Lord? Your answers to these questions will determine your experience in the supernatural realm and the sensitivity of your spiritual vision. In Revelation 3:18, the Lord even advised the Laodicean church to buy "eye salve" that they might see.

What are you seeing? In other words, what do you know because of the Spirit, or what are you perceiving as He gives you insight? Faith will see according to God's perspective. We can train and sensitize our spiritual vision by meditating on the Scriptures, allowing our vision of life, Heaven, and the spiritual realm to be renewed by His Word. His Word carries final authority. If you see it by revelation in His Word, then you can believe for that blessing to be manifested in your life. Deuteronomy 29:29 says, *"The secret things belong to the Lord our God, but the things revealed belong to us and to our sons forever, that we may observe all the words of this law."*

One time as I was speaking with a Christian minister and sharing some Scripture about our position in the heavenly places, I became so excited and testified how I had encountered regular experiences in the heavenlies simply by entering through faith into the reality of the promises of God. He was somewhat disturbed concerning my revelation and experiences and challenged me, saying, "I just don't see it and I don't believe it." I was somewhat caught off guard for a moment until the Holy Spirit rose up within me and gave me insight.

"You can't see it?" I asked as I pointed the Scripture to him once again. He replied, "No, I cannot see what you see." I replied with respect for him and yet with conviction, "Well, I guess if you can't see it, you can't have it. I, however, do see it and am enjoying the experience of it." If it is not revealed by the Spirit of God, you cannot "see" it. God will often conceal things until we are ready to receive—until we are hungry. Sometimes, our academic understanding of the Scriptures can block those things the Lord desires to show us, those things that are hidden deep within the verses, those things that true seekers can find. I have discovered that as I ask God for deeper revelation of His glory, He gives me more. He satisfies the hungry soul, but hides revelation from those who don't desire it. I simply approach Him with childlike faith and a pure heart. Open our eyes, Lord, to fresh revelation of Your truth every day. Perhaps that is why Paul prayed for the church at Ephesus,

> That the God of our Lord Jesus Christ, the Father of glory, may give unto you the spirit of wisdom and revelation in the knowledge of Him: the eyes of your understanding being enlightened; that ye may know what is the hope of His calling, and what the riches of the glory of His inheritance in the saints, and what is the exceeding greatness of His power to usward who believe, according to the working of His mighty power (Ephesians 1:17-19).

# Faith Speaks

We always speak what we believe. Jesus said, *"The mouth speaks out of that which fills the heart"* (Matt. 12:34b). The spoken word is very powerful and creative when it carries the breath of the Lord in it. Jesus said that the words He spoke were spirit and life (see John 6:63). *"By faith we understand that the worlds were prepared by the word of God"* (Heb. 11:3a). When we confess or proclaim the truth about the Kingdom realm, it begins to build a framework in the spirit and will literally have effect upon our lives.

## *Daily Confessions*

As I mentioned earlier, I make it my habit to make confessions of the Word of God daily. I speak out the word of blessing over my life, marriage, children, friends, ministry team, and church. I confess the promises because I believe the promises. Begin to confess the Word of God out loud on a regular basis and you will find yourself strengthened in truth and sensitive to the spirit realm. Blessings will begin to come upon you and overtake you.

For example, confess by faith that every time you enter into the "tent of meeting" (your devotional time with the Lord), the glory cloud descends upon you like it did for Moses. Jesus said that the glory the Father had given Him, He gave to us (see John 17:22). Continue to speak out that truth and you will be amazed at the eventual outcome. The promise will manifest. You will then most likely begin to actually sense the glory of God in your body and emotions. At first you might not feel or sense anything, but simply continue to lock in to the promise by faith and confess the truth of the Word. You can count on His promises; they are your inheritance in Christ.

Here's an application. Do you desire to "experience" the presence of the Lord in His throne room? Then it's time to hear a word from God. Ask the Spirit to quicken His Word to you, then begin to perceive the promise of God through the eye of faith. Ephesians 2:6 clearly states that we *"sit together in heavenly places in Christ Jesus"* (KJV). Where is Jesus? On the throne! (see Eph.1:20-21). Then where are you, if you are indeed "in Christ"? Dare you declare it? All spiritual experience must be led by the Holy Spirit and based on the truth of the Word of God. If the Word says that you are in the "throne zone," then you are! Your spirit man is already positioned.

Hebrews 4:16 encourages us to boldly come to the throne of grace so that we can obtain mercy to help in time of need. Do you believe this promise regardless of whether you feel it or sense it? Then, confess it. Speak it out: "Thank You, Jesus, that I am at the throne of grace. I have accessed the throne room and am receiving help, grace, and mercy in my time of need." Why would we confess that? Simply because the Word says this is true and we believe it. Faith speaks, and the more we speak out the Word of God in faith, the more we will see its manifestations. We will review these principles again in another chapter so you can be anchored in the concept of accessing the Kingdom realm by faith. This is so important.

You might be thinking, *how can we just confess something and then think it is real?* Kingdom truth is already real and eternally true. Your confession doesn't make it real; your confession is an expression of faith. Let me share with you a simple example that you might relate to. Let's first examine the following Scripture from Romans 8:8-10:

> *But what saith it? The word is nigh thee, even in thy mouth, and in thy heart: that is, the word of faith, which we preach; that if thou shalt confess with thy mouth the Lord Jesus,*

*and shalt believe in thine heart that God hath raised him
from the dead, thou shalt be saved. For with the heart man
believeth unto righteousness; and with the mouth confession
is made unto salvation.*

According to this portion of Scripture we see:

1. The word of faith is in our heart.

2. If we confess that Jesus is Lord and we believe in our
   own heart that God raised Him from the dead, we shall
   be saved.

3. With the heart man believes unto righteousness.

4. With the mouth confession is made unto salvation.

Now then, when are we saved? Do we need to wait to enjoy this
new life of Christ within, or does He enter at the point of re-birth?
Are we a new creation at the moment we believe, receive, and confess; or does this new creation come alive later through some sov-
ereignly appointed angelic messenger, dream, or visions or maybe
five dreams and three visions…hmm…maybe after two angelic
encounters?

According to the Scripture, when we confess and believe, we
are saved. The night I gave my heart to Jesus was an unforgettable
night. I believed. I confessed. Since that time I have been enjoying by faith my salvation experience on a daily basis because I am
saved now. I have had some glorious sovereign encounters from the
Lord, angelic visitations, and exciting heavenly experiences, but I
don't live for them. I live for Him because I believe! My salvation
is not based on supernatural, sovereign encounters. My salvation
is real. It is true. Why? Because the Bible says so. That is enough
for me. It is tangible through faith. Nothing could be more real to
me. I love exploring the depths of my salvation package through

journeys in the Scriptures as the Holy Spirit reveals eternal truth. This is a daily walk and a daily encounter! Faith.

I constantly speak of the glories of the Lord whether I experience the reality of them in the natural or not. I choose to live in the eternal reality of the truth of God. I believe, therefore I speak! I confess that I am forgiven, that I am righteous, that I am loved with an everlasting love. Do I feel forgiven all the time? No. In the natural, I feel condemned at times. Do I feel righteous all the time? No. I clearly see that I have sinned and fallen short of the glory of God in my natural life. Do I constantly feel that I am loved with an everlasting love? No. Sometimes I feel like a big disappointment to Him. How I feel though is not what is true. His Word is truth. He is truth, and He says that I am forgiven, righteous, and loved with an everlasting love. Because I believe the reality of that, I confess it. When I confess it, I activate the reality of it within my life, and the manifestation of these marvelous truths begins to unfold beautifully within the realm of time. Confession is what activates your faith.

## Faith Endures

Galatians 6:9 declares, *"Let us not lose heart in doing good, for in due time we will reap if we do not grow weary."* When you desire to enter into experiencing the spiritual realm, you need to be committed to standing on the truth of covenant promises, even at times when you feel spiritually dull.

In the last chapter, I shared my testimony of how I was called to live the truth in my spirit by faith, even when everything in my circumstances, emotions, and body felt shut down. Although the truth regarding the tangible glory presence of God had not yet manifested in my life, it was still truth. I locked in to the truth and endured until the promises manifested in the natural realm.

We often give up in our faith walk when it looks like the promise is never going to manifest. Yet God wants us to endure and stand in faith even when things don't look like they are lining up with His promises. Abraham endured even though, in the natural, his wife was beyond childbearing years.

Many heroes of faith found in Hebrews chapter 11 went to their graves still believing even while not receiving the manifestation of the promise, but they went home in faith, while the promise of the Messiah manifested in the "fullness of time." It was the faith of these heroes that made the connection for that ultimate "download." They believed right up until their last breath this side of time. They carried the truth in their hearts by faith, never doubting throughout their lives; and their faith greatly pleased the Lord. Faith endures.

## Faith Receives

Faith also receives the reality of the promise, even before it is manifested in the natural realm. *"Therefore I say to you, all things for which you pray and ask, believe that you have received them, and they will be granted you"* (Mark 11:24).

All the covenant promises regarding the glory realm are secured into our lives by faith. Faith is different from hope. We are not hoping to have experiences in the unseen Kingdom realm. We believe that we are in the realm of His Kingdom because the Word says we are. There is a big difference. Hope never secures the promises. Faith does. The receiving dimension of faith is literally how we lay hold of the blessings.

I remember hearing a testimony a number of years ago from an acquaintance of ours. Her 11-year-old daughter had been learning from her Sunday school teacher how to receive by faith. The child asked her mother one day if she could have a piano because she wanted to worship Jesus with it. Her mother explained that they couldn't afford a piano at the time; however, she encouraged her daughter to pray.

The daughter went into her room and prayed a simple prayer: "God, I know that You've got lots of pianos in Heaven, and so I was just wondering if You could give me one?" She remembered Mark 11:24, a Scripture verse she had learned in Sunday school. She firmly believed that when she prayed, she received. Following her time of prayer the child ran out to share her exuberance with her mother. "Mommy, Mommy, God just gave me a piano." "He did?" her mother inquired. "Where is it?" "Oh, it is in my spirit," replied her little girl. "I have received a piano from God by faith." The mother was touched by her daughter's adorable behavior and imaginary piano. She thought no more about her daughter's confession and did not actually take the faith project that seriously.

A few days later, the family went to church. Following the service, the church pianist approached the daughter, saying, "Honey, this week was my birthday and my husband bought me a new piano for a present. I was going to sell my old one, but as I was praying about it, I felt the Lord move my heart to give it to someone as a gift. I believe He said I was to give it to you. Can you use a piano?" The little girl was excited and blessed but not at all surprised. She had already received her piano before it manifested. She had learned the powerful lesson that "faith receives."

This is a simple illustration, but it is an example of how to secure all of Heaven's blessings for your life. When you pray, believe that you have received, and you will have what you believe if it is according to the promises of God.

You don't need to cry out and say, "Oh Lord, if only I could have a heavenly experience, if only I could experience being in Your Presence, if only I could experience Your power." No. These things that you desire are already promises that God has given you in His Word. All you need to do is receive the reality of these things into your life by faith. Walk in them by faith. Faith receives. If you can grab hold of the revelation of this teaching on faith, then a spiritual revolution is sure to fill your life.

## Soaking and Receiving by Faith

A dear friend of ours, Todd Bentley, is a young, fiery evangelist who has discovered a powerful way to receive. He grew up in very difficult and tragic circumstances and, in his early teens, was involved in crimes and confined to a juvenile penal institution for a season. Todd was then transformed by the power of the Lord's saving mercy when at age 18 he found Christ. Immediately, he received an evangelistic passion. He was hungry for everything that the Lord had for him. He daily devoured the Word of God and became intimately acquainted with the Holy Spirit. Todd was full of fire and still is!

After a few years of serving the Lord, Todd had to take time off work due to a job-related injury, so he determined to use his free hours to seek the Lord. He now refers to this period as his "soaking season." For hours every day he would play a worship CD and sit before the Lord and soak. He has testified that at times during the first number of hours he would not feel the Lord's presence, but he decided to continue to wait on the Spirit, believing that he was receiving of the glory of God. He soaked in faith and eventually received of the substance of heavenly glory. By faith, he was "drinking out of a glory well." Jesus said in John 7:37b, *"If anyone is thirsty, let him come to Me and drink."*

Day after day, he would seek the Lord in this fashion. Before long he was experiencing heavenly encounters, visions, and heart-to-heart dialogue with the Father. Today, Todd continues to spend time each day soaking in the presence of God and receiving the glory by faith. As a result, Todd is passionately ministering salvation, healing, deliverance, and signs and wonders to the multitudes all over the world. He simply ministers out of what he sees his heavenly Father do in Heaven. How? By faith.

Without faith you will never be able to see God, and you will not experience the Kingdom realm. But with faith, all things are possible. Only believe. Faith truly is the connector to the invisible Kingdom realm and to heavenly glory. And during this spiritual revolution, God's people will launch into Kingdom assignments and miraculous signs and wonders through the operation of their most holy faith!

## Chapter Six

# THIRD-HEAVEN ENCOUNTERS

I haven't always had understanding and experience concerning heavenly realities. Actually, I remember years ago when I first heard the term "Third Heaven." A young minister had exclaimed with great enthusiasm over the telephone one day, "Hey, Patricia, I've been having awesome times with God in the Third Heaven lately!"

Sometime afterward, I started hearing this curious term, "Third Heaven," along with testimonies of related experiences, more and more often. Back then, I had seemed to be growing in spiritual sensitivity and openness to the Holy Spirit's leading into divine encounters, but this young man implied that Third-Heaven encounters could easily be an everyday occurrence for every believer. My heavenly experience in 1994 had come through a sovereign visitation, but could things like this actually be experienced on a regular basis? His suggestion of such a possibility piqued my curiosity and stirred my spiritual hunger. I also felt a certain "fear of the unknown" as well as some godly caution. I had many questions and, at that point, very few clear answers.

My personal questions and concerns about believers accessing Third-Heaven experiences took me on a journey through the Scriptures. Day by day, the Holy Spirit revealed increased measures of understanding regarding the invisible Kingdom realm and how we as born-again believers have access to that realm.

## What Is "The Spiritual Realm"?

The spiritual realm in Scripture is the unseen, invisible, and eternal realm. *"While we look not at the things which are seen, but at the things which are not seen: for the things which are seen are temporal; but the things which are not seen are eternal"* (2 Cor. 4:18 KJV). Although the spiritual realm is invisible, it is very real. In fact, the spiritual realm is actually more real than the natural realm. The natural realm is that which is within time. It is what the Scripture calls temporal or subject to time.

I often think of *time* as a substance in eternity like a small capsule placed inside of a massive and endless expanse. In the light of all eternity, time is very small. We spend only a few years within the time realm, and the Scripture teaches us that it is like a vapor. Our life within time is extremely short in comparison to eternity, and we have only one opportunity to live within it. Natural and physically tangible things are experienced within this realm.

Overlaying this physical, natural realm is an invisible zone called the spiritual or unseen realm. As we already discovered in Second Corinthians 4:18, the things that are invisible are of the eternal dimension. If you were to sit in a kitchen of a friend's home, you would be able to describe the things that you see and sense in the natural realm. You might describe the refrigerator, stove, dishwasher, chairs, table, and dishes. If the host was baking some bread in the kitchen, you might also describe its wonderful fragrance. Your natural senses would be aware of the natural surroundings.

In this same kitchen there is also an invisible sphere, a spiritual dimension not discerned by the natural man but discerned by the spirit. It is invisible to the physical senses, but it is truly real and is tangible to the spirit. The spirit realm overlays the natural realm in the earth and below the earth, and it extends through the earth's atmosphere even to the highest Heaven.

It is possible, while living in the realm of time, to have discernment in the realm of the spirit. In Second Kings 6:13-17, we read the account of Elisha praying for his servant's eyes to be opened to "see" into this unseen realm. It is obvious in this passage that Elisha himself was familiar with this spiritual dimension. In the natural realm it looked like they were outnumbered by their enemies, but when they saw through the eyes of their spirit, they could see the host of Heaven, chariots, and fire all around them. Elisha was confident that there were more with them than there were with their natural enemies because he saw into the invisible realm. So also did his servant after he prayed for him. You can too.

The Scripture clearly describes two kingdoms within the spiritual realm—the Kingdom of God and the kingdom of satan. In Matthew 12:22-28, Jesus teaches about the reality of these two kingdoms. Colossians 1:12-13 also confirms the idea of two kingdoms in the unseen realm. As believers, we are citizens of the Kingdom of light, a Kingdom that cannot be shaken. Glory to God! We are on the winning team!

The demonic realm is also real and so are the evil spirits that abide in this dark kingdom. But although satan's kingdom is real, it is defeated. Christ Himself defeated the devil, and therefore, we have been given power over all the power of the enemy when we are in Christ (see Luke 10:19). We never need to fear a dark spirit, not even satan himself.

In God's Kingdom, Jesus has rule. The God-head, believers, and celestial beings dwell within this Kingdom. The Bible also describes beautiful attributes within this realm, like love, righteousness, peace, and joy. It is a glorious Kingdom of power, might, and awesome splendor, and the moment we receive Christ we are translated out of darkness into this Kingdom.

## What Is "The Third Heaven"?

The Third Heaven is a place in God's invisible Kingdom realm. Paul introduces the term "Third Heaven" in Second Corinthians 12:2. *"I know a man in Christ who fourteen years ago—whether in the body I do not know, or out of the body I do not know, God knows—such a man was caught up to the third heaven."*

Genesis 2:1 confirms the idea of a plurality of heavens when it says, *"Thus the heavens and the earth were completed, and all their hosts."* Scripture also speaks of a place called the highest heaven: *"Behold, to the Lord your God belong heaven and the highest heavens"* (Deut. 10:14a).

If the Bible says that there is a Third Heaven, the inference then is that there is a first and second heaven as well. It seems that the first heaven is the heaven that displays the stars, sun, moon, and earth's atmosphere (see Ps. 8:3). Although purely speculative, the second heaven (which is not actually a biblical term but is titled by inference) is believed by many Bible scholars to be the realm from where the demonic hierarchy rules. Daniel chapter 10 describes a wrestling between a high-ranking celestial being (possibly Jesus or a high-ranking angel) and the principality of Persia.

Apparently, this warfare took place in the second heaven. Although the second heaven might be the place where demonic strategies and hierarchy operate from, it is not owned by the devil. All the earth and all the heavens are under Christ's authority. The second heaven also has angelic activity taking place within it. It is not solely the devil's realm, even as the earth isn't. With all this being said, it is important to note that any interpretation of the second heaven is purely speculative.

Many of today's Christian leaders believe that the Third Heaven contains the throne room of God as described in Revelation chapters 4 and 5, and Isaiah chapter 6. Ephesians 1:20-23 makes it very clear that Christ is seated on a throne far above all other principalities, powers, names, and titles. It is the place of God's abode.

Some Christians believe there are higher levels than the Third Heaven and that the Third Heaven is not necessarily the throne room level. They propose that the Third Heaven is what Paul refers to as the *"paradise of God"* in Second Corinthians 12:4 and that there are still higher realms beyond. Although this theory could possibly be true, the Bible makes no clear, specific reference to any levels of Heaven higher than the third. Any suggestions of higher realms would be "extra-biblical." Although such an idea is not necessarily "anti-biblical," it is always wise to stay within the boundaries of the Scriptures when it comes to spiritual experience.

If you want to know what Heaven is like, you can find it described in the Scriptures. Explore Third-Heaven glory, discovering things like the appearance of King Jesus Himself, His throne, the living creatures, sapphire streets, the crystal sea, and the glorious rainbow, by meditating on Isaiah 6:1-8; Ezekiel 1; Daniel 7:9-10; Exodus 24:9-11; and Revelation 1:10-16; 4; 5; 19:1-16; 20:11-12; 21:1–22:7. The Scriptures give us such an amazing glimpse of Heaven.

## Ascending and Descending

In Genesis 28:12, we find that Jacob had a dream. In this dream he saw a ladder set up on the earth with the top reaching to Heaven. Angels were ascending and descending on it. Many believers, including children, experience the ascending and descending dimensions of Third-Heaven encounters. Is this valid and is it scriptural?

We see Jesus in John 5:19-20 explaining to His disciples that He did only what He saw His Father do. We know through Christ's teaching that our Father lives in Heaven (see Matt. 6:9). It appears that Jesus engaged in encounters with His Father in Heaven and then downloaded strategies into the earthly realm. He did only what He saw His Father do. We know that Jesus historically ascended in Acts chapter 1, but according to John 5:19-20, we see that He devotionally ascended regularly also.

In Exodus chapters 24–34, we see that Moses ascended the mountaintop and engaged in divine and heavenly encounters. On one occasion, he even ate and drank in Heaven, along with the 70 elders of Israel while beholding God on sapphire streets (see Exod. 24:9-11), and then descended, bringing the commandments of the Lord to the people. In chapter 34, we find that even his physical countenance was influenced by the presence of the Lord's glory in the heavenlies. As he descended into the camp, His face shone so brilliantly that it had to be veiled to protect the people from its intensity.

The prophet Isaiah, in Isaiah chapter 6, ascended in a vision to the throne room of God and saw the Lord high and lifted up and His train filling the temple. He also saw the seraphim and engaged in a life-changing encounter. He was then sent back into the earthly realm newly commissioned.

John and Paul are other Bible characters who ascended into heavenly visions and encounters and then brought the revelation to the people in the earth. They were ascending and descending.

## *Who Can Ascend and Descend?*

We have just seen through the Scriptures that Jesus, His angels, and Old and New Testament believers have ascended and descended. Believers today can also ascend and descend. If you are a believer in Christ, you can access the Third-Heaven dimension by faith and receive a throne room perspective. You can also bring into the earthly and natural realm the revelation you receive in the heavenlies in the same way as Paul, John, Isaiah, and others did in Bible days. Christ Himself is the true Jacob's ladder into the heavenlies. Jesus said to Nathanael in John 1:51, *"Truly, truly I say to you, you will see the heavens opened and the angels of God ascending and descending on the Son of Man."* Jesus is the ladder. He is our way of ascending and descending into the heavenlies.

## Spirit, Soul, and Body

In a previous chapter, we covered the topic of the functions of the spirit, soul, and body and new creation realities. This is an important topic in which you must have full understanding when it comes to Third-Heaven encounters. Once you comprehend the revelation of your born-again spiritual nature and the functions of your body, soul, and spirit, it makes it easier to understand heavenly encounters. So, let's review.

When you were born again, it was your spirit that was born again. Jesus said in John 3:6, *"That which is born of the flesh is flesh, and that which is born of the Spirit is spirit."* At the point of being born again, Christ's Spirit enters your human spirit and you experience new birth. When you were born again, your spirit man became a new creation. Second Corinthians 5:17 says, *"Therefore if any man be in Christ, he is a new creature: old things are passed away; behold, all things are become new"* (KJV).

You see, it is not your body and soul that are born again. It is your spirit. Your spirit man comes alive with the very nature and character of Jesus Christ at the time of your rebirth. You become filled with Him and are given all that He has (see 2 Pet. 1:3). At that moment, you entered into the eternal and unbreakable covenant that Jesus secured for you on the cross. All the blessings in the heavenly places are yours according to Ephesians 1:3. You are absolutely perfect and complete within your born-again spirit nature.

Your born-again spirit is already familiar with the heavenly dimension and the realm of the Kingdom of God. Remember, your spirit is eternal in nature. If you understand and believe this reality, it is not too difficult to see how you can enter that spiritual door into divine encounters. You must learn to walk in your new spiritual nature by faith and pray for your soul and body to be awakened to the unseen Kingdom realities. You are one with Christ in your spirit and there is no time or distance in the eternal dimension. You can be living in the earthly realm in your physical body and yet at the same time be positioned in the heavenlies.

## Come Up Here

John, in Revelation 4:1, was given an invitation to enter the throne room. The Scripture says, *"...and behold, a door standing open in heaven, and the first voice which I had heard, like the sound of a trumpet speaking with me, said, 'Come up here, and I will show you what must take place after these things.'"* John was shown an open door into Heaven and then the voice instructed him to "Come up here!" The voice didn't say, "I am going to bring you up here." Somehow John had to respond to the command to "come." If I invite you to come to my house, I do not mean that I am going to bring you to my house. You need to respond to the invitation if you want to come. Faith is the connector with which John responded. That is how you encounter the Lord in the realm of the unseen dimensions of the Kingdom of God. It is through faith responding to the faith connection.

Colossians 3:1-2 exhorts us with the following: *"Therefore if you have been raised up with Christ, keep seeking the things above, where Christ is, seated at the right hand of God. Set your mind on the things above, not on the things that are on earth."*

Many times, I have heard Christians say, "You can get so heavenly-minded that you are no earthly good. While I understand that this saying most likely addresses those who might be imbalanced, that is not what Colossians 3:12 says. This passage actually strongly exhorts us to seek those things above and to set our affections and passions there.

In addition, Hebrews 4:16 encourages us to *"draw near with confidence to the throne of grace"* in order to receive mercy, grace, and help in time of need. Where exactly is the throne of grace? Could it be in the Third Heaven? If so, we are urged in the Scripture to "come boldly."

Carefully read the following Scripture passage:

*For Christ did not enter a holy place made with hands, a mere copy of the true one, but into heaven itself, now to appear in the presence of God for us. ... Therefore, brethren, since we have confidence to enter the holy place by the blood of Jesus, by a new and living way which He inaugurated for*

*us through the veil, that is, His flesh, and since we have a*
*great priest over the house of God, let us draw near with a*
*sincere heart in full assurance of faith...* (Hebrews 9:24;
10:19-22).

Wow! Read that passage over again and again until you understand this clearly. Do you see the revelation this portion offers?
Jesus has made a way for us through His blood to access Heaven
now. We are given the invitation to enter the holy place and to draw
near with full assurance of faith.

## Sovereign Act or Faith?

A sovereign act is completely initiated by God Himself and
has nothing to do with man's ability, determination, or initiation. It
is solely a divine intervention. Often the Lord performs sovereign
acts among His people to initiate His purposes. It is like an intro-
duction to what He is about to manifest and establish in the earth.

The outpouring of the Spirit in the first chapter of Acts is an
example of this. Before His ascension, Jesus told His disciples
that the promise of the Spirit was coming. They postured themselves in prayer in order to birth this promise, but they didn't have
a clue what the event was going to look like. The Holy Spirit came
in divine timing and by a sovereign move of God. Filled with the
Holy Spirit, they all began to speak unknown languages. What a
surprise to find each other speaking in these new languages which
they had never previously learned. The believers who had gathered did not enter into the experience of speaking in tongues by
faith, rather the experience entered into them.

*There is a difference between the promise of God coming to you*
*and you going to the promise.* Sometimes, in prophetic ministry,

the Word of God will *come to the prophet*, while at other times, *the prophet will seek the Lord* for the Word.

We can see a similar sovereign principle at work in the area of pastoral ministry. At times, the Lord will spontaneously drop the Sunday morning message into the pastor's spirit. The pastor doesn't even need to prepare or study it. The inspiration comes directly to his heart from God. Most of the time, however, he will need to seek the Lord for the message. He will need to study and access the message by faith. One is a sovereign act, and the other is by faith. Which one is more valid? Neither. Both are valid. They can both be pure and powerful messages from God, but they are received in different ways.

The Scripture does not say, "The just shall live by God's sovereign acts." It does state though, *"The just shall live by faith"* (Rom. 1:17b KJV). Most believers seldom experience a sovereign act of God. For the average Christian, it is a daily walk of faith through which they access the promises in the Word of God. All the promises have already been secured for us in Christ (see 2 Peter 1:3-4). The table of the Lord's blessing has already been set. We simply need to access the promises by faith.

Sometimes individuals actually believe that God will impose His gifts on people against their will. A number of years ago, after I shared the gospel with a woman, she replied in this manner: "If God wants me saved, then He will save me." However, it is not a question of whether God wants her saved. He does. And He has already secured her salvation 2,000 years ago through Christ's death on the cross. His work of salvation will not benefit her, though, unless she accesses it and appropriates it by faith. The same is true for all Kingdom promises. Jesus said, *"I came that they may have life, and have it abundantly"* (John 10:10). In John 17:24, Jesus prayed, *"Father, I desire that they also, whom You have given Me, be with Me where I am, so that they may see My glory which You have given Me."*

Wow! That sounds like a Third-Heaven invitation and promise to me. Are we willing to access it by faith as we follow the Holy Spirit's leading? Will the Lord give some individuals a sovereign visitation to the Third Heaven? Perhaps, but what if we never experience a sovereign encounter? Are we able to visit the glory realms of Heaven by faith as the Spirit directs and enjoy valid spiritual experiences? What do you think?

## Keys to the Heavenly Realm

All of our spiritual experience must be based on the authority of God's Word and His covenant promises. Again, recognize that all the promises and blessings in the Word are ours in Christ. Many are spooked by the thought of an individual having a Third-Heaven experience, and most believe it is only for a few very special people. Personally, I would like to see all the spookiness and the exclusiveness removed from Third-Heaven experience. It is quite simple to understand. Our born-again spirits are already one with Heaven. We don't have to really go anywhere. We are already there! We are already in the throne room. The Word says we are in heavenly places (see Eph. 1:20-23; 2:5-6). We simply need to acknowledge this truth by faith. If the Word says that we are seated with Christ in the heavenly places, then we are! There is no argument. The Word says it...we believe it. No mysticism. No spooks. No hoping to go. We are just there! Truth says so, whether we feel it or not, and through our faith we acknowledge the truth concerning our spiritual position in the heavenlies.

Spiritual revolutionaries are aware of the importance of this Kingdom reality and are aware of the importance of living from a heavenly perspective and dimension. Now, would you like to know how to help your soul and your body become more familiar with what is already real in your spirit? Would you like to know how to connect the truth and the reality of heavenly encounters into your emotional, mental, and physical experience? Do you want to enjoy a more intimate relationship with the Holy Spirit? Well, then, follow me into the next chapter.

Chapter Seven

# THE HELPER (OR THE GUIDE)

How well are you acquainted with the person of the Holy Spirit? Are you aware of His presence as you go about your day? Do you listen for His counsel? Are you familiar with what pleases Him and what displeases Him? The Holy Spirit is committed to leading and guiding everyone into all truth, but more than anything else, He desires relationship with you. Paul refers to this as communion with the Spirit (see 2 Cor. 13:14). He will teach you all about the Third Heaven and how to enjoy spiritual experience within the boundaries of the truth. He will never lead you into error for He is the Spirit of truth (see John 16:13).

When you ask Jesus to come into your life, it is His Spirit, the Holy Spirit, who enters you. He comes and indwells your human spirit and gives you new life (see John 3:3-6). He is within you right now if you have received Christ as your Savior, and within Him are all His gifts.

In Acts 1:5, Jesus prophesied to His disciples that they would be baptized with the Holy Spirit. The word *baptize* means to be fully immersed or to be completely filled. When you ask the Lord to baptize you in the Spirit (which is a subsequent experience to salvation), you are actually inviting the Holy Spirit's presence to fill your soul and body, as well as your spirit man where He already resides. In this way, you are completely immersed in Him; this is actually an act of consecration, or being set apart for God.

In addition to asking for an initial infilling of the Spirit, we can also ask for a refill whenever we need one. Ephesians 5:18 says, *"Be not drunk with wine, wherein is excess; but be filled with the Spirit"* (KJV). The word "filled" here is written in a present, ongoing tense. In other words, it means that you can get filled, and filled, and filled! Take time, right now, to get acquainted with the Holy Spirit. He is so lovely. Invite Him to fill you to overflowing with His holy presence in your body, soul, and spirit. He will! It is important to have your soul and body filled with the Spirit when you desire to experience heavenly encounters.

Now, remember, don't allow your feelings or lack of them to determine if your experience is valid. You are filled because you have asked and He has answered. The Scripture says so! (See Luke 11:13.)

Following are 70 functions of the Holy Spirit found in the New Testament. He is in you and with you to perform these duties:

1. He leads and directs. Matthew 4:1; Mark 1:12; Luke 2:27; 4:1; Acts 8:29; Romans 8:14.

2. He speaks (in, to, and through). Matthew 10:20; Acts 1:16; 2:4; 13:2; 28:25; Hebrews 3:7.

3. He gives power to cast out devils. Matthew 12:28.

4. He releases power. Luke 4:14.

5. He anoints. Luke 4:18; Acts 10:38.

6. He comes upon/falls on. Matthew 3:16; Mark 1:10; Luke 2:25; 3:22; 4:18; John 1:32,33; Acts 10:44; 11:15.

7. He baptizes and fills with. Matthew 3:11; Mark 1:8; Luke 1:15,41,67; 3:16; 4:1; John 1:33; Acts 1:4-5; 2:4; 4:8,31; 6:3,5; 7:55: 10:47; 11:24; 13:9,52; 1 Corinthians 12:13.

8. He gives new birth. John 3:5,8.

9. He leads into worship. John 4:23.

10. He flows like a river from the spirit man. John 7:38-39.

11. He ministers truth. John 14:17; 15:26; 16:13.

12. He dwells in. John 14:17; Romans 8:9,11; 1 Corinthians 3:16.

13. He gives comfort, health, and strength. John 15:26; Acts 9:31.

14. He proceeds from the Father. John 15:26.

15. He shows us things to come. John 16:13.

16. He gives the gift of tongues. Acts 2:4.

17. He releases prophecy, dreams, visions. Acts 2:17,18; 11:28.

18. He transports. Acts 8:39.

19. He brings direction, guidance. Mark 12:36; 13:11; Acts 10:19; 11:12; 21:11; 1 Timothy 4:1.

20. He is holiness. Romans 1:4.

21. He is the Spirit of life, and gives life (*zoe*). Romans 8:1,10.

22. He invites us to walk with Him. Romans 8:4-5.

23. He groans, prays, and intercedes. Romans 8:26-27.

24. He is a Sword (the *rhema*). Ephesians 6:17.

25. He produces fruit. Galatians 5:22-23; Ephesians 5:9.

26. He helps us in weakness. Romans 8:26.

27. He bears witness. Acts 5:32; 15:28; 20:23; Romans 8:15-16; Hebrews 10:15; 1 John 4:13; 5:6-8.

28. He is the Spirit of adoption. Romans 8:15.

29. He gives power to mortify the deeds of flesh. Romans 8:13.

30. He provides power for signs, wonders, preaching. Acts 1:8; 1 Corinthians 2:4.

31. He ministers love. Romans 15:30.

32 He searches deep things of God. 1 Corinthians 2:10.

33. He quickens the mortal body. Romans 8:13.

34. He brings revelation. Luke 2:25; 1 Corinthians 2:10,12; Ephesians 1:17-19; 3:5.

35. He reveals to us what has been given by God. 1 Corinthians 2:12.

36. He washes, sanctifies, purifies, justifies. Romans 15:16; 1 Corinthians 6:11; 2 Thessalonians 2:13; 1 Timothy 3:16; 1 Peter 1:2,22.

37. He has gifts. 1 Corinthians 12:4-11; Hebrews 2:4.

38. He seals us. 2 Corinthians 1:22; Ephesians 4:30.

39. He is liberty. 2 Corinthians 3:17.

40. He changes us into the image of Christ. 2 Corinthians 3:17.

41. He is the promise of the blessing of Abraham. Galatians 3:14.

42. He releases a cry to the Father. Galatians 4:6.

43. He gives access unto the Father. Ephesians 2:18.

44. He builds us together for a habitation for God. Ephesians 2:22.

45. He strengthens us with might. Ephesians 3:16.

46. He is unity. Ephesians 4:3-4.

47. He is wine. Ephesians 5:18.

48. He supplies. Philippians 1:19.

49. He is fellowship. 2 Corinthians 13:14; Philippians 2:1.

50. He is grace. Hebrews 10:29.

51. He is glory. 1 Peter 4:14.

52. He speaks to the churches. Revelation 2:11,17,29: 3:6,13,22.

53. He calls for the Bridegroom. Revelation 22:17.

54. He has the power of conception and anointing for God's purposes. Matthew 1:18,20; Luke 1:35.

55. He teaches. Luke 12:12; John 14:26; 1 Corinthians 2:13; 1 John 2:27.

56. He gives commandments. Acts 1:2.

57. He provides power to be a witness (martyr). Acts 1:8.

58. He provides boldness. Acts 4:31.

59. He gives sight. Acts 9:17.

60. He commissions. Acts 13:4.

61. He restrains. Acts 16:6.

62. He appoints ministries/gives authority. Acts 20:28.

63. He releases love. Romans 5:5.

64. He is righteousness, peace and joy. Romans 14:17; 15:13; 1 Thessalonians 1:6.

65. He confesses Christ's Lordship. 1 Corinthians 12:3.

66. He brings the Gospel. 1 Thessalonians 1:5-6.

67. He is keeping power. 2 Timothy 1:14.

68. He brings renewal. Titus 3:5.

69. He moves on believers. 2 Peter 1:21.

70. He convicts the world. John 16:8.

Isn't He amazing? And He is God's gift to you and will help you live a godly life while you are here on earth. He is the one who fills you with Kingdom power, miracle-working power, and makes you a mighty witness in the earth. We must learn to know Him and then follow His leading. And in order to follow Him, we must be familiar with how He speaks to us.

## The Subtle Ways the Holy Spirit Speaks

The Bible reveals a variety of ways that God speaks to His people, including audible voices, open visions, trances, dreams, and angelic visitation. The most common way the Holy Spirit speaks, however, is through what we call, "God thoughts" and "God impressions."

I have the privilege of being in relationship with many seasoned and respected prophets—ministers who prophesy global events and warnings, weighty words for the Body of Christ, and who have experienced amazing visitations, open visions, trances, and audible voices at times. They have admitted, however, that the most common way that the Spirit speaks to them is through the still small voice in the mind and faint impressions in the imaginations. They also have disclosed that most of the time words from the Lord come to them as they are seeking God and posturing themselves to hear from Him. We often have the impression that in order for a word to be really significant, it must come in a thundering voice or in an open trance vision that comes to us from out of the blue. This is not normally the case. Even Elijah, a very powerful prophet in Bible days, heard God speak significantly to him in the still small voice (see 1 Kings 19:12).

In order to follow the leading of the Spirit, we need to hear His voice and then obey. Kingdom encounters are always led by the Holy Spirit and are always walked through by faith.

## Faculties of the Soul

Remember, your spirit man is already fully alive and in touch with Kingdom realities from the time you are born again. Your spirit is the part of you that is sensitive to the spiritual life around you, and it is through your redeemed spirit that you are able to have intimate relationship with God.

Your soul, however, is the part of your being that houses faculties such as the mind, will, emotions, passions, and imaginations. The soul expresses and experiences the relational dimension of your life and needs to understand Kingdom reality in order to connect relationally with God on emotional and intellectual levels. In order to build a strong relationship with someone, interaction in the area of intellect, emotion, passion, vision, and communication are extremely important.

When born again, your spirit is already in complete relationship with God, His Word, and His ways, but your soul needs understanding so that the conscious part of you can experience God and the invisible realm. The Holy Spirit helps us while we live on the earth to understand with our soul the ways of God so that we can make conscious choices to follow and serve Him. Your will, which is part of your soul, is the decision-making part of your being.

If you were to peel off your body and your soul and have only your spirit man left, you would be fully aware of the invisible Kingdom and spiritual realm. That is the nature of your spirit, but your soul needs to receive information and revelation in order to have relationship with God and in order to relate to others in the world around you.

How, then, can your soul receive input from the Holy Spirit so that you, within the realm of time, can be sensitive to the invisible Kingdom of God? What part of your soul can receive this type of revelation that gives entrance into experience? If the spiritual realm is invisible, then how can you relate with your natural and soulish senses?

## The Mind

Your mind was created in you so that you would have the ability to reason and to think God's thoughts. In Isaiah 1:18, God invites His people to "Come, let's reason together." You will find that most of the Holy Spirit's leading is through Him speaking into your thoughts.

Your mind is the organ of your soul that processes these thoughts and plays a very important function in Kingdom experiences. Your thoughts can come from a number of sources, and each thought needs to be discerned as to what source it is coming from, including:

1. **Your own carnal nature.** These thoughts are usually selfish and are not God-centered.

2. **The world.** The world system has a strong voice. For example, on the television media, you might find the voice of the world saying that you are acceptable as a man only if you have a great muscular build and you are an acceptable woman only if you have a slim, trim figure. The spirit of the world speaks concerning its own standards, which are usually not in line with God's.

3. **The demonic.** The devil will attempt to speak lying thoughts into your mind that are contrary to the Word of God. His voice is usually condemning, accusing, and enticing. Even Jesus, in Matthew chapter 4 was tempted by the devil.

4. **God.** When the Holy Spirit authors thoughts in your mind, they are always according to His Word, His ways, and His nature.

When God created your mind, it was never His intention for you to use this important organ of the soul for evil purposes. Your mind is never to house evil, lustful, or proud thoughts. It is to be set apart for God to use, to communicate His purposes to you, and then in turn, you can make wise decisions and build a strong relationship with Him. Unfortunately, due to the fall, our mind has been filled with all kinds of evil things over the years. But if we want the Holy Spirit to use our mind to speak to us, then it is important that we cleanse it from every ungodly thought and that we watch over our thinking processes. We want our mind to be a vessel that is sanctified for the Holy Spirit's use.

Continually ask the Lord to forgive you for every evil thought, and then be cautious and selective with what you allow your mind to be filled with. Be careful what you listen to. For example, if you listen to lustful music all day long, your mind will become polluted with lust, which will hinder your ability to hear the Holy Spirit with accuracy. It is like having rust in water pipes. The water might be pure coming from the reservoir, but the rust in the pipes will contaminate the water when it travels through those pipes and out the faucet. This is true concerning your soul as well. Hence, you are exhorted in the Scripture to watch over your heart with all diligence because from it flows the issues of life (see Prov. 4:23).

One way that you can prepare your mind to hear from the Holy Spirit is to season it by meditating on the Scriptures. Read the Word and then think on it, ponder it. Invite the Holy Spirit to give you special insights and fresh revelation. This will renew and help your mind to receive the authority that is in the Scriptures and will prepare your soul to receive the quickened and inspired Word that comes from the Holy Spirit.

Another way you can bring your mind into greater submission and sensitivity to the Spirit's leading is to ask Him questions and then wait on Him for the answer. This is especially effective when you journal both your questions and your answers. Then test your answers against the authority of the Scriptures and the nature of God to see if the Word is true. Following is a simple example:

**Question:** Lord, do You love me?

Wait on the Lord for the answer. The answer comes into your thoughts.

**Answer:** Yes.

**Question:** How do You love me?

Wait on the Lord for the answer.

**Answer:** With an everlasting love.

Now, take those answers and search the Scriptures for confirmation. Do these answers line up with the Word and with His nature? According to Jeremiah 31:3, we know the above example lines up with both the Word and His nature. This confirms that we have heard the voice of the Lord. The more you submit your mind to hearing God's thoughts and then confirming those thoughts, the more sensitive to His voice you will become. Keep a journal and practice listening for His voice every day.

## The Sanctified Imagination

The imagination is another organ of the soul and when cleansed by the power of the Spirit has great potential. Imagination is the ability to see what is not yet perceived or present to our knowledge. It is the part of you that receives vision. God is a visionary, and so are you, for you were created in the image and likeness of God. While imagination is prized for its role in artistic creativity and human understanding, it is also condemned for its link with false images.

So often, the imagination is downplayed or disrespected. We often believe that if something is of the imagination, then it is not real. This is not true. Again, it is very important that we know the source of the inspiration. Our imaginations were never created in us for ungodly, sinful, or vain impressions, but for God's holy purposes. The Word clearly communicates that without a vision, we will perish (see Prov. 29:18). We need vision, and the imagination is the organ that permits us to receive that vision.

In every type of spiritual vision, the imagination is engaged. This is true of trance, open vision, dreams, and faint impressions. But without the imagination in use, you have no vision at all. In addition, a vision can be revisited because it is backed up in the memory bank of your imagination, or vision center.

The most important thing to understand about the imagination is that it needs to be sanctified in order to operate as a doorway for your faith to engage the invisible realm of the spirit. Your imagination is the organ the Holy Spirit uses to transmit spiritual concepts to your soul. Unfortunately, we often allow vain and lustful pictures to fill our imaginations.

Just as we ask the Lord to forgive us of our unclean thoughts, we need to do the same with our imagination. We need to pray for the imagination to be set apart for the Holy Spirit's use. Be very careful to watch over what your eyes feast on. Remember, the images you see with your natural eyes will paint a picture in your soul. Television, movies, and magazines these days often reveal things that our imagination should not be submitted to seeing.

After the imagination is cleansed and set apart for God, you can strengthen it by submitting it to the visions within the Scriptures. The visions found in the Books of the prophets, for example, carry prophetic authority in them. Submit your imagination to the images in the Scripture and allow the authority of the

Word to unlock pictures within your soul. This will season your visionary receptivity. Ask the Lord to allow you to envision that particular scene in Scripture. Envision the power of the scenery and the passion of the heart. Try to see yourself within that particular situation, and ask yourself how you would respond or act. As you do this, an environment will be created in which God will be able to speak to you. Once again, remember that you are to allow the Holy Spirit to lead and inspire you. Submit yourself to Him. Your imagination is not leading you; rather it is the Holy Spirit Himself who is filling you with divinely inspired impressions. Your imagination is simply an organ that He can use to bring heavenly inspiration when you submit and yield to Him.

## "Practicizing"

In Ephesians 1:17-18, Paul is praying for the Lord to give the believers at Ephesus the spirit of wisdom and revelation in the knowledge of Christ. He also prays that the *"eyes"* of their *"understanding"* be enlightened (KJV). In Strong's Concordance, we find that the Greek word used here for "understanding" is *dianoia*. This word is rendered as "mind," "understanding," and "imagination" within the Scriptures. Paul is actually praying for the eyes of the imagination or the eyes of the mind to be opened to comprehend supernatural things.

As we have already explained, much of our spiritual revelation is fed into our image center (imagination) or our mind. This is the place where you will often "see" visions of glory, and it is the Holy Spirit who enables you to see visions or impressions of the glory realm. God also reveals heavenly glory by releasing holy ideas, counsel, and understanding into your thoughts.

Many believers are not open to receiving spiritual experience in the imagination or thoughts, yet those are the places where you will actually receive most of your spiritual inspirations. And if you will allow those organs of the soul to be used by the Holy Spirit, you will begin to enjoy more spiritual visions and encounters.

Hebrews 5:14 states, *"But solid food belongs to those who are of full age* [mature]*, that is, those who by reason of use* [practice] *have their senses exercised to discern both good and evil"* (NKJV). "By reason of use" refers to practicing or exercising the ability. You can "practicize" (practice and exercise) your spiritual senses by filling your mind with images and concepts from the Word of God. "Practicizing" is actually acting on what you believe. James 2:17-18 gives us an important key to acting on the Word or practicizing. *"Even so faith, if it has no works, is dead, being by itself. But someone may well say, 'You have faith and I have works; show me your faith without the works, and I will show you my faith by my works.'"*

Some believers become very upset about the concept of practicing or exercising spiritual abilities, and yet, the same people have no difficulty with other things such as music ability. Here is an example: A young man wants desperately to become a worship leader and would love to lead by using the keyboard. Most Christians would expect this spiritual gifting to be developed through learning some theory, daily prayer into the goal, disciplined practice on the instrument, and by taking every opportunity to lead worship—activities that would cause growth in anointing and skill as a musician and worship leader.

Likewise, we would expect a person who desired to be a skilled intercessor, to attend prayer seminars, study the subject from the Word of God, and practice, practice, practice. You don't become a skilled intercessor by only attending a seminar on the subject but by actually doing it. The more you pray, the more seasoned you become. And furthermore, in order to become a good prayer warrior or a seasoned worship leader, you must not wait until you feel the urge to pray or to practice your instrument. The honing of your gift comes from discipline and much practice. If you waited for the urge to practice, you might never engage.

The same goes for anointed soul winning. The more you share the Gospel, the more you unlock that anointing. It is a principle. Acting on the Word of God is important to grow in any gift, be it healing, prophecy, or administration. Practice makes perfect! Why then are we afraid to engage our mind and imaginations in spiritual strengthening and practice? Why is this any different?

When you enter into Third-Heaven experience, your encounters will be led by the Holy Spirit as He uses your mind and imagination to reveal glorious revelation and encounters. Let's get over the unwarranted fear of seasoning the organs of our soul that facilitate the revelations from God. There are those skeptical individuals who argue that because the New Age practitioners use the imagination and mind, we shouldn't. Remember, the enemy is a counterfeit. He is aware of which organs connect a person to the reality of spiritual life and activity. It is all about source, not about function. God created the mind and imagination (creativity) as portals for divine experience. The questions are: Who is leading the experience? Who is the source?

Chapter Eight

# PITFALLS AND ACTIVATION

Spiritual encounters in the heavenly realm should be quite normal for born-again believers. However, the language used to describe these heavenly experiences often tends to make these encounters sound unattainable or impossible for the average person.

Even so, it is God's desire for all His children to enjoy spiritual experience under His direction. And the more you exercise your spirit toward God-encounters, the more natural they will become.

## Avoiding the Pitfalls

Many fear the unknown and in particular the thought of experiencing the invisible realm. They believe it is dangerous and should be avoided so that one does not fall into deception or error. Are there possible dangers in this school of spiritual experience? Most definitely, yes! Any time a person lives outside the perimeters of the Word, way, or will of God in any area of their lives, danger is lurking.

Likewise, in your natural life, there are things that could be dangerous if you do not abide by proper principles. For example, driving a car can be extremely hazardous if you do not abide by the laws of the road. But if you read the owner's manual, abide by the rules, exercise caution, and watch out for the other guy, you will most likely maintain a safe and successful driving record. Meanwhile, the inherent dangers of driving should not deter you from getting in your vehicle and heading for your destination.

I oftentimes face resistance from individuals regarding the possibility of entering into invisible Kingdom encounters. They say, "It is best to stay away from that stuff because you could step into deception with it." Interestingly, those same believers don't seem to possess the same connectivity in their spiritual antennas when they want you to enter their churches that hold to forms of godliness but deny the power (see 2 Tim. 2:5). In any case, it is very important to know any elements of spiritual danger or deception.

Following are some examples of dangers that one should be aware of before getting in the "driver's seat" of spiritual experience.

## Witchcraft and Occultism

Any activity or manipulation of the spirit realm not under the rule of Christ is called witchcraft. This practice is forbidden in Scripture. Be careful of "guided imagery," a practice in which someone else tells you what to see. This can lead to manipulation (see Deut. 18:10-14; Gal. 5:17-25). The Holy Spirit is the only one who can lead you into divine encounters, not another individual or another spirit. If you have had previous experience with New Age, false religions, or the occult, you will need to fully renounce those practices along with any spirit guides or spiritual counselors who taught you. This is very important. You need to be cleansed from all that is false and submit to all that is true. If you have had previous involvement with counterfeit sources, then pray the following prayer:

> *In Jesus' name, I renounce all occult and New Age practices including _____ (specifically mention practices you ere engaged in). I also renounce all books, recordings, and paraphernalia used in these practices. In Jesus' name, I renounce all rituals, rites, baptisms, ungodly vows, and covenants; and I cut all ungodly soul ties with counselors, Gurus, covens, occult priests, teachers of spiritual practices, spirit guides, and New Age medical practitioners. Forgive me, Jesus, for my involvement in these things and cleanse my spirit, soul, and body from the influence. In Jesus' name, I serve eviction notice to any and every demonic spirit that has entered me as a result of such involvement. I command them all to leave in Jesus' name. Fill me now, Lord, with your precious Holy Spirit. I will submit only to You, for You, Lord Jesus are my God, my Savior, and my King. Amen.*

## Idolatry and Unhealthy Fascination

Our primary passion must always be for the Lord Himself, and we must always place Him at the center of our affections. All spiritual experience needs to draw the heart and affections of the believer to deepened relationship with Christ; however, we must avoid being overly fascinated with spiritual experience. John, in Revelation 19:10, fell into deception when he began to worship the heavenly being that brought him the vision. John was the closest disciple to Jesus' heart and yet even he was in danger of deception. Beware.

## Experience Orientation

Although we clearly mentioned in a previous chapter that God desires us to experience Him and His Kingdom in order to build relationship, when believers focus only on spiritual experiences, it can cause great problems with both their walk and character. They can begin to believe that their spiritual encounters are endorsements of their character and maturity. This is not the case. Love, true worship of Christ, as well as faith and obedience to the Word of God are the real hallmarks of authentic Christian living.

## Pride and Self-Exaltation

No one is beyond being tempted with pride. Lucifer himself, even though he was the covering cherub over the ark and a high-ranking angel in Heaven, fell into the sin of pride. That sin cost lucifer his place in Heaven, and he was cast out!

Simon Peter is a classic example of how pride and self-rule can begin to rise up even right in the midst of a divine encounter. While on the Mount of Transfiguration, he said, "Lord, it is good for us to be here" and arrogantly told Jesus what they should be doing (see Matt. 17:4).

The apostle Paul was also aware that he was susceptible to pride because of the *"abundance of revelations"* he received (see 2 Cor. 12:7). If these Bible figures could be in danger, it is vital that we also guard against pride. A good accountability team is helpful and necessary. Remember, pride is a deception you cannot observe in yourself. Listen to others and clothe yourself in humility and teachability!

## Touched but Not Changed

Christ's powerful ministry of healing the sick, cleansing lepers, raising the dead, and liberating the oppressed touched Israel for over three years. Yet at the end of his ministry to them, He wept, saying, *"If you had known in this day, even you, the things which make for peace! ...You did not recognize the time of your visitation"* (Luke 19:42,44).

The nation had been powerfully visited by the manifest *dunamis* (miracle-working power) of God, and yet those who gathered in His final hour cried, "Crucify Him!" They were touched but not changed.

When you receive a powerful touch from the Lord's hand, it says nothing about you. It doesn't endorse your character or your ministry. It does, however, say something about the Lord. It says He is mighty! He is loving and merciful!

If I were to lavishly give a million dollars to a friend, the kind gesture says nothing about my friend. It does say something about me though, perhaps that I am generous. We will learn something about my friend, however, once she does something with the money. Whether she uses the gift to build homes for the homeless or sets up a prostitution ring, either act will say something about her. Heavenly encounters have the potential to enrich and empower a believer's walk, but they are not a guarantee. The manifest goodness of the Lord is to bring blessing, repentance, and enrichment to our lives, but there are no guarantees that our response to

His acts of kindness will reveal a changed life. May we be touched *and* changed!

## Error and Deception

Entering into spiritual experience without a proper and complete foundation in the Word of God can sometimes open the door to error and deception. Good solid Bible teaching should always accompany spiritual experience. Our Glory Schools teach students with this goal in mind. If you see a vision or enjoy an encounter in the glory realm, then study it out in the Word of God afterward. Always let the Word of God be the first testing place to validate experience!

As we mentioned earlier, it is also important to have a good accountability circle around you and some mature Christians who can help mentor and pastor you into maturity. In the multitude of counselors, there is wisdom.

# Daily Disciplines
# to Experience the Invisible Kingdom Realm

Our experience in the invisible Kingdom realm is led by the Holy Spirit and is born out of relationship with Him. Daily spiritual discipline is advantageous in that it helps us to position ourselves before Him and to focus our attention on His goodness toward us. The Bible teaches us to be disciplined and to bring our flesh under submission to the Spirit. Discipline fortifies our will and develops our character, but it does not produce an encounter. Experience in the glory is never *earned*; it is simply a gift, granted by His grace and goodness and received by faith.

We can, however, always anticipate the manifestation of the goodness of the Lord when we posture ourselves to receive.

*Then Moses said, "I pray You, show me Your glory!" And He said, "I Myself will make all My goodness pass before you, and will proclaim the name of the Lord before you..."* (Exodus 33:18-19).

Following are daily disciplines, principles, and preparations to enhance worship, surrender, and experience in heavenly glory.

1. Acknowledge that you are born again. It is your spirit that is born again, and in your spirit you have the very nature of Christ. You are one with Christ for all eternity. This new birth is a gift to you, and it cannot be earned. It is received by faith; it is the gift of eternal life, the life of Christ. You have the nature of Christ; you are forgiven; you are holy; and you are full of wisdom, righteousness, and power.

Meditate on and confess all that you are and all that you have in your born-again spirit. This is the true *you*. Your spirit man is to rule over your soul and body and is not to be subdued. Bless your spirit man and set it apart to fulfill your Lord's purposes.

In my booklet and CD entitled *Decree*, there are scriptural confessions concerning your new nature. I personally attempt to make a daily practice of declaring out loud these statements of faith concerning who I am in Christ. This helps me to define my born-again spiritual nature as I am a new creation in Christ; old things have passed away and all things have become new (see 2 Cor. 5:17).

If you are not yet born again, then give your heart to Jesus right now. Remember that the Source of your experience is everything. Invite Him, in simple words, to come into your life and forgive your sins. He will! If you have been involved in any New Age or occult practices, renounce them and ask the Lord for cleansing. You can say the prayer in the previous section.

2. Choose to lay down the rule of your soul life. Call your carnal nature crucified. Submit your soul to the rule of Christ. Confess that your soul delights in submitting to the rule of Christ. Declare that your soul will not make its own decisions nor follow its own inclinations.

3. Receive cleansing and forgiveness through the blood of Jesus for any area of your life that has transgressed the will and nature of God. All your sins are forgiven when you humbly confess your transgressions before Him. They are removed as far as the east is from the west. Confess that sin does not have dominion over your spirit, soul, or body. Declare that you do not serve sin but you serve your God and all that He represents.

4. Consecrate your body, soul (including mind, will, emotions, imagination, affection), and spirit to the purposes of God. Submit your entire being to the glory of God. Declare that your physical body is a container that reflects heavenly glory and that your entire being is fully influenced by the glory and presence of God.

5. Like Moses, enter the "tent of meeting" by faith. This is a time and place that you set apart each day to meet with God. During these times, choose to completely focus

on the Lord and allow all the agenda and the busyness of the day to be laid down. Choose with expectancy to meet with Him.

6. Acknowledge your deep love and reverence for the Holy Spirit. He is your guide, your teacher, your helper, and your comforter. He leads you into all truth and comes alongside of you to bring you into fruitfulness. Allow Him to lead you daily into worship of Jesus and into glorious Kingdom experiences.

7. A wonderful gift of the Holy Spirit is the gift of tongues (see 1 Cor. 12:10; 14:2,4; Acts 2:4). This gift will help build you up in your most holy faith and edify your spirit man. You will find that daily and focused prayer in tongues will help you to be more spiritually sensitive. As you pray in tongues, you declare the mysteries of the Kingdom of God and proclaim His mighty deeds.

8. Drink of the glory of the heavenly realm by faith. Jesus said in John 7:37 that if we are thirsty, we can come to Him and drink. How do we drink of Him? By faith. When you drink something in the natural, you swallow; you draw in the liquid and allow it to fill your belly. This is the way you drink of the Lord, His love, His wisdom, and His truth too. Soak in His presence and draw His love into your heart and life. Be filled. The Holy Spirit will lead you in this. Drink daily of the Lord's goodness and allow your soul to receive all that is in the deep well of your spirit.

9. Study the Word daily and seek to know God in deeper ways. Invite the Lord to give you fresh revelation of

the Word. It is a lamp unto your feet and a light unto your path. You will not stumble when you obey His Word. If you abide in Him and His Word abides in you, then you will be fruitful and experience answers to prayer. The Word will be a garrison around your mind and will keep you within the truth.

10. Worship Jesus in spirit and in truth. Acknowledge His worth and His value. Proclaim the glorious truth regarding your God, and knit your heart together with Him in intimate love. The highest and holiest respect of your life belongs to Him and to none other. Behold His beauty and glory and exalt Him to the highest place in your life.

11. Engage in devotional and intercessory prayer while in His presence. Share your heart with the Lord and make your needs known to Him. Pray for the needs of others as the Holy Spirit directs and believe for the advancement of His Kingdom in the earth. A strong prayer life will cause you to be acquainted with His heart and purposes.

12. Wait on Him. Rest. Listen. Watch. Wait in expectancy for Him to bring fresh revelation and insight. Savor His presence and delight in what He shows you. Record in your journal the treasures that He reveals and meditate on these things throughout the day. Respond to the things your heavenly Father shows you. Jesus said, *"...the Son can do nothing of Himself, unless it is something He sees the Father doing; for whatever the Father does, these things the Son also does in like manner"* (John 5:19). Obey His leadings and commit yourself to walking throughout your day in His glory realm.

These disciplines will help keep you focused on the Lord and on who you are in Him. Whatever you focus on, you will empower. Daily disciplines prepare your heart for heavenly experience.

## Would You Like a Heavenly Encounter?

The way I personally enter into heavenly encounters is to first submit myself and all my faculties to the Holy Spirit's guidance. I then begin to worship Jesus and follow the Spirit's leading. Sometimes, He leads me through little thoughts in my mind or impressions in my imagination. My thoughts and imaginations do not lead me, but they can be used by the Holy Spirit to speak to me concerning what He desires to reveal when I submit those faculties to Him. I look to Him alone, not my own carnal thoughts, imaginations, worldly values, or demonically sourced inspiration. I declare, "The voice of a stranger I will not hear!" (see John 10:5). I choose to believe what He shows me no matter how faint it seems. To me, every revelation is a spiritual reality. So often, we discard thoughts and images because we think they are inspired through our unredeemed soul. Some folks say things like, "Ah, that is just me!" But if we submit ourselves completely to the Holy Spirit and pray for Him to lead us into divine encounters, then we must believe that He does.

Many Christians have spiritual and heavenly encounters, but they don't identify them. This is often because they believe that to have a valid encounter it must look, feel, and sound according to their own expectations. Some people do not believe they have encountered the Third Heaven, for example, unless they have a trance vision and hear the audible voice of God. Even though the Holy Spirit might be giving them faint impressions and thoughts regarding the throne room, they do not believe this to be a valid experience.

Do you understand that the still small voice can carry as much if not more authority than the audible voice of God at times? Do you know that the faint visual impressions the Holy Spirit gives you are not a lower level of revelation than an open vision? I have experienced the audible voice of God and open trance visions on occasion, and they have been a blessing both to myself and to those I have shared them with. But some of the most significant and fruitful spiritual revelations I have received were actually through God-thoughts and God-impressions—very faint ones I might add. It is not what type of vision or revelation you receive that makes it significant or not. Many visions and encounters that are seemingly subtle and dull actually can bear enormous fruit. Do not despise that which appears insignificant. Your faint impressions are as valid as an open vision. Lean into all the Holy Spirit gives you and embrace it as true spiritual reality.

At times, your natural mind might struggle to accept what the Holy Spirit reveals to you. First Corinthians 2:14 teaches us that *"But the natural man does not receive the things of the Spirit of God, for they are foolishness to him; nor can he know them, because they are spiritually discerned"* (NKJV). Sometimes the natural man thinks that God should give the revelation in a certain way, but the Lord is the one who chooses the ways He reveals His Kingdom to His people, and as a result causes us to walk in faith and obedience and not by sight or senses.

## Accessing the Realm of the Spirit Through the Word of God

As we have previously mentioned, the Word of God is not merely print on a page or an expression of language. The Word of

God is an eternal, spiritual substance. The words of Jesus are "spirit and life."

Another way I personally enter heavenly encounters is to simply believe what the Word says and enter into the life of the Word as a spiritual reality. As a covenant child of God, you can choose to access the promises. For example, if you desire to get saved and you receive revelation concerning salvation, you don't have to wait for an angelic visitation or a special audible voice from Heaven to invite you to give your life to Christ. On the basis of the Word itself, you can respond. This is the same for all Kingdom encounters. Responding to the Word of God is a doorway into Kingdom encounters.

## Believe Beyond Doubt

The greatest enemies to spiritual experience are doubt and unbelief. It was unbelief that kept Israel from entering the Promised Land. They doubted because they believed more in their outward circumstances rather than on the promises God gave them. The outward circumstances were tangible to their natural senses, while the promises were invisible. They chose to believe what their natural senses could absorb, thereby denying the invisible promises.

Oftentimes, our minds will say, "That's not a spiritual experience; that is just my mind." Of course, the mind, imagination, and feelings are involved in spiritual experience, but if it is the Holy Spirit inspiring you, then the thoughts or impressions become a connection to the invisible. If you have prayed for the Holy Spirit  to lead you, then don't doubt after you pray. Believe that He is in the lead. The more you believe in faith that you are being led by Him, and embrace what you see as a true connection into the unseen realm, the more you will experience in the glory. Faith is a key, whereas doubt is an annihilator. To doubt makes us double-minded, according to the Book of James, and unstable in all our ways. James further says that a double-minded man will receive nothing from the Lord (see James 1:6-8).

In our Glory Schools, we teach students online how to follow the Holy Spirit into heavenly encounters. Our subsequent course, The Glory to Glory School, is a full two days of activation into the glory realm. Students are taught how to trust the Spirit's leading, and they often gain great confidence as their doubts are shattered. Most say following the training, "I didn't know it was so simple." Walking in the realm of heavenly glory is so simple that even children find it easy. If you desire to enter into heavenly encounters, then pray the following prayer with me and get ready to receive.

*Heavenly Father,*

*Thank You for allowing me bold access into the throne room. Thank You for creating in me a spirit that is able to relate to the spirit realm. I invite You to grant me rich and meaningful spiritual experience in Your presence so that my walk with You and my mission in the earth might be enriched. Fill me with a spirit of wisdom and revelation in the knowledge of Christ.*

*I submit myself to You, Holy Spirit, and will follow You into glorious experiences in the Kingdom. I release my heart to You now. Fill me with Your glory! Draw me into intimacy with You and grant me an awareness of my position with Christ in the heavenly places and the invisible Kingdom of God. In Jesus' name. Amen.*

Now, focus on Him, the heavenly realm, His glory, and enjoy. If you sense nothing at all, remember that your *spirit* is engaged in divine encounters even if your *soul* is not aware of the experience. Remain in faith and thanksgiving. Expect great things. A new door of opportunity in Christ has opened.

Chapter Nine

# LIGHTNINGS AND DRAGONS

During our first year of full-time global itinerant ministry, my husband and I were seldom at home (we are actually at home even less now). After returning from one of our ministry trips, we decided to invite some of our prophetic friends over for an evening of fellowship and to get a pulse on what the Lord was saying to them and to our region.

As the time approached for our guests to arrive, I was preparing some coffee and goodies when the Holy Spirit spoke to me and said, "I don't want you to share with each other, pray, communicate visions, or even worship unless I direct you. Be still and wait for My unction." Well, that was a surprise. I had anticipated a rather exciting evening of sharing and fellowship, and now it sounded like God's agenda was possibly one of stillness and quiet meditation.

As already mentioned, one of the most important keys to spiritual experience is to submit yourself completely to the leading and guidance of the Holy Spirit. He is our Helper and Teacher. He directs us into all truth and is our personal Mentor in spiritual experience as we get to know Him. He is not a mere influence or power, but a Person. He is the Spirit of God!

Comprehending all of this, I submitted to His direction that evening, even though I did not understand it. As our guests came, we greeted them, and when all had arrived, I shared what the Holy Spirit had spoken. I instructed, "Let us not pray, sing a song, prophesy, share a vision, or even read a Scripture unless the Holy Spirit directs. We will simply wait on Him. If, however, He does nudge you to initiate something, then go for it."

Waiting on the Lord is quite a discipline because, most of the time as Christians, we are not comfortable with stillness and quietness. We tend to want to say something to break the silence. However, that evening, we all agreed wholeheartedly to follow His leading. Isaiah 40:31 states, *"Yet those who wait for the Lord will gain new strength; they will mount up with wings like eagles, they will run and not get tired, they will walk and not become weary."* (Note: Eagles are often a symbol of prophetic ministry and unction in the Scripture.)

As we were waiting, it wasn't long before someone felt led to pray, then someone else was inspired to sing a song. The Spirit's presence rested on us, and as we followed His leading, we enjoyed a very sweet time of fellowship and began to flow in prophetic unction under the noticeable weight of His glory.

## Lightnings!

As we continued to submit ourselves completely to His leading, suddenly a vivid flash of light came from the center of the ceiling in the room. Oh my goodness. What was happening? "It's lightning!" I exclaimed loudly, but we were inside the house. We all acknowledged it...well, all but one.

Someone in our group, who wasn't actually a prophetically sensitive person (but was there to serve the group that evening) said, "It's probably a short circuit in the electrical system. There is a light fixture in the center of the room, and maybe it just flickered from an electrical short."

Although the rest of us were all convinced that it was lightning and an actual visitation from God, we agreed to honor the "skeptic." And in order to eliminate any room for further doubt, we turned off the ceiling light, allowing only a couple of table lamps and a few candles to remain lit and illumine the atmosphere.

As we continued to wait on the Lord, another bolt of lightning flashed in the same place where the first had appeared. Yikes! We were being visited by a divine sign and wonder! Despite our excitement, the skeptic continued to question the phenomenon. "Well, what if it's still an electrical short and the table lamps are reflecting the light flash?" Skeptics are great, aren't they? They put our faith to the test, and that's good for us!

So, to further test this experience, we turned off the lamps, leaving the candles as our only source of light. We continued to wait on the Lord, and before long, another lightning flash lit up the room, and then another, and another. There were about six in total that evening, and our excitement rose to fever pitch.

As we continued to wait on the Holy Spirit, He gave us insight into the lightnings of God. Lightning in the natural supposedly brings order to ions (electrically charged particles) in the earth's atmosphere. This act in nature clears and freshens the air. Lightning also changes the molecular structure of soil. Farmers apparently welcome lightning because it causes planted seed to grow faster. Lightning will also strike the "highest place" and will often destroy whatever it hits. Hmm...could this characteristic of lightning be a prophetic picture of the destruction of pride, the clearing of the spiritual atmosphere and the accelerated growth of the seed of the Word in the soil of our hearts? The Lord revealed many more things to us regarding His lightnings and gave us prophetic applications. We were then led into a prayer time to release His lightnings into His Church.

Since that night, we have encountered other visitations of His lightning, thunder, and other spiritual phenomena. In Revelation 4:5a, the Scriptures confirm that in the throne room there is lightning and thunder. *"Out from the throne come flashes of lightning and sounds and peals of thunder."* Other Scriptures confirming the lightnings of God are Revelation 8:5; 11:19; Exodus 19:16; 20:18; and Psalm 97:4. In Jeremiah 10:13; 51:16; and Psalm 135:7, we see the lightnings of God in relation to the rain. Rain is often a sign of revival. Perhaps the Lord is sending the supernatural prophetic sign of His lightnings prior to fresh outpourings of His Spirit.

I have often seen in open visions, what is referred to as objects of light or "orbs." In the Miriam-Webster Online Dictionary, the definition of an *orb* is "a spherical body; especially: a spherical celestial object." The orbs our team has seen are like circles of light that vary in size and color. At times, we have seen them in our television camera shots and in photographs. On one occasion, we magnified a photo of some orbs that were seen in one of our conferences. It was amazing as it revealed a large blue light orb that had "wheels within wheels." Many Christians are seeing these manifestations of light; however, some have challenged us saying, "Orbs are of the New Age." This, of course, is not true.

We must look at the source. It is possible that a circle of light that shows up in digital photography could be as a result of a light refraction. This then would not be a supernatural phenomenon but rather a natural phenomenon. If a circle of light, however, is

created and manifested by God then it would fall in the category
of a sign and wonder. It would make you respond in awe of God.
I usually find that my spirit is quickened and stirred when it is a
sign and wonder. The Scriptures teach that our God is *"the
Father of lights"* (James 1:17). He is the Creator of all things. He
is the Creator of light. Those involved in New Age practices are
usually very spiritually sensitive, so they can probably see things
in the realm of the spirit. Discernment is always needed to determine the source of a supernatural manifestation. The Bible does
say that satan attempts to disguise himself as an angel of light
(see 2 Corinthians 11:14). It is therefore possible that counterfeit
demonic spirits can also manifest in various forms. As believers,
we have been given the gift of the discerning of spirits so that we
can easily tell the difference. The more we spend time in the
presence of God who is perfect Light, the easier it will be to discern the false. The lightnings, orbs, and thunders of God are very
real in the unseen realm. Our hearts came into a deeper awakening concerning these things that evening as we simply waited on
Him with worshipful focus.

## Another Wave

After a while, the tangible presence of the Lord seemed to
wane, and I thought that perhaps we could break for coffee. (I do
have a particular fondness for coffee...only blessed and sanctified
coffee though, of course!) Just as I was about to make the suggestion, one of our friends said, "I feel the Lord saying that if we continue to wait on Him, He will give us another wave of visitation."
All right! That beats coffee any day, even if it is sanctified! This is
a powerful point to ponder. Too often, we don't wait long enough on
the Lord. We leave a prayer time or spiritual encounter quickly

and miss the next level of what the Lord desires to do in our life. Tarrying is very important and is found all throughout the Bible.

We continued to wait on the Lord that night, committed once again to respond only to His direction and not to our own desires. As we followed His nudging, the tangible weight of His presence began to visit us once again. Unexpectedly, I proceeded to speak out in the gift of tongues. I wasn't praying in tongues; it felt more like preaching in tongues.

The unknown tongues sounded like some type of Chinese dialect. One thing was for certain, though, I had never spoken in this language or in this fashion before. Others in the room began to join me, most of them speaking in various types of oriental-sounding syllables.

## The Dragon

After preaching in tongues for a while, I was suddenly aware that, in my spirit, I was in a Chinese village in Mongolia. I can remember the hillside vividly to this day, as well as the little homes and the dusty main pathway through the hamlet. I remember seeing people going about their daily routine. I also saw into the spirit realm over the village. A very large, ferocious, green-colored dragon was hovering over the settlement and seemed to take its position right over the main street or pathway. I discerned that this dragon was a ruling demonic spirit in this region in Mongolia and was enslaving this village under the power of deception and control.

The dragon could not see me. I was above it, preaching up a storm in these "new tongues" with tremendous fervency and confidence, and I could literally feel the strength and might of the Lord as I spoke. When God calls us to spiritual warfare, He wants to give us a heavenly perspective. It is a good thing to be above and not beneath when facing dragons. Right?

We have already established in previous chapters that Jesus is positioned in the highest Heaven, far above all principality and power, and has put all things in subjection under His feet. We have also clearly established that we are seated with Him in the heavenly places. In this experience, I was clearly above the dragon spirit while making powerful warring decrees in unknown tongues.

In the vision, I suddenly saw the dragon lose strength. It was as though the words in tongues were actual arrows penetrating its life source. It fell to the ground and appeared to die. Finally, in the vision, I witnessed a tremendous outpouring of the Spirit fall over the region, and the entire village came to Christ. The peoples' eyes were opened to see the truth. Through this experience, the Lord revealed that a battle had been won in the heavenlies and that harvest would break out for a season in Mongolia. Many in that nation would come to Christ during a season of grace.

Since that time, I have become acquainted with ministries that preach the gospel in Mongolia. They have reported amazing divine encounters in this country where a great harvest of souls is taking place with demonstrations of God's power in specific regions of the nation.

When you are in a heavenly vision or trance, the Lord gives prophetic interpretation and understanding of what you are experiencing. Sometimes the interpretation comes during the vision, and at other times, there is a need to seek the Lord for more understanding and insight following the encounter.

After this engagement in prophetic warfare, I shared the vision with my friends who were in the room, and we prayed for more insight from the Holy Spirit. As in this situation, the Lord will sometimes take us into spiritual experiences to engage us in high-level strategic intercession and warfare.

Since that event, I have had other confrontations with dragons. One was in Taiwan during a ministry trip. In the midst of a worship session one night, the Lord showed me a vision of a golden dragon that represented the spirit of mammon over that region. The Lord gave me wisdom on how to preach truth through my message that would release His people into conquering faith. Many of them had been oppressed by the influence of this dragon spirit. They began to pray and repent at the end of the message, and then supernatural things started breaking out in the meeting. Many people received gold glitter all over their hands. A young boy threw a golden-colored, satin altar cloth up to a 30-foot ceiling, and it stuck flat against the ceiling for about 40 minutes. He then asked the Lord to make it fall down, and it immediately did. These were signs to the people present, indicating that the Lord's glory and power were exalted above the power of dragon. The next day, we were able to lead souls to the Lord in the public restaurant. This was part of the spoil. Within a week of that incident, our television program was signed on in Asia to broadcast in seven nations, including Taiwan. More of the spoil!

Before that evening in our living room, I had never heard of people sharing dragon stories, even though I realized that the Scripture is full of evidence of the reality of dragons. For example:

> In that day the Lord will punish Leviathan the fleeing serpent, with His fierce and great and mighty sword, even Leviathan the twisted serpent; and He will kill the dragon who lives in the sea (Isaiah 27:1).

*And there was war in heaven, Michael and his angels wag-
ing war with the dragon. The dragon and his angels waged
war* (Revelation 12:7).

About a year or so after the event in our living room, a missionary friend of ours shared a story of a young Christian in Nepal, who
traveled into remote areas and won entire villages to the Lord.
Subsequently, other missionaries in the area questioned him as
they had not experienced any breakthrough with the gospel in
those demonically oppressed communities. "How did you do it?"
they asked.

"Oh," he replied in his simple faith. "It was easy. I just slew
the dragon first." He had grown up in this oppressed region and in
his unsaved state was very aware of these spiritual demonic entities that threatened the people. When he came to the Lord, slaying the dragons just seemed like the right thing to do with the
authority he had in Christ.

I realize that some of you right now are probably silently
screaming with resistance to this concept. There has been a great
deal of teaching in the Western church that promotes fear concerning demonic entities. We have been taught that believers in Christ
have no right to address spiritual wickedness in the heavenlies.
Although I totally believe we need to exercise caution in this arena
and I appreciate much of what is taught within that mind-set, the
Scripture does say, *"Thou shalt tread upon the lion and adder: the
young lion and the dragon shalt thou trample under feet"* (Ps.
91:13 KJV). Remember that we are positioned in Christ and all
things are under our feet when we are in Him. Did you notice in
Psalm 91 that the instruction was to trample under our feet, and
not shoot up into the heavens from the earth? Position in the spirit is important.

## Considerations

In Ephesians chapter 6, Scripture instructs us that our warfare is against spiritual entities and not flesh and blood. A believer should never presume, however, to fight a spiritual battle outside of the direction of the Lord of hosts, our Commander and Chief. Caution definitely needs to be exercised when engaging in spiritual combat. Any battlefield, whether in the natural or the spiritual, is not a playground.

Believers have, however, been given *"authority over all the power of the enemy"* (Luke 10:19) and should never be afraid of any level of demonic spirits, not even satan himself. Colossians 2:15 makes it clear that through Christ's victory, all demon powers have been defeated and disarmed. Matthew 28:18 informs us that all authority in Heaven and in earth has been given unto Christ. Note carefully that the Scripture says Christ's authority is in Heaven as well as the earth. We have authority in Him!

Although the truth about our authority in Christ is clear, we should never enter spiritual battles outside of the Spirit's endorsement and leading. The devil indeed comes to steal, kill, and destroy, but we must also remember that Jesus came to give us life and that in abundance (see John 10:10).

Many excellent teachings regarding intercessory warfare and its treacheries are readily available at this time. It is strongly advised to gain good foundational teaching on spiritual warfare and acquire tight accountability before engaging in it. I believe that the government and the authority of the Kingdom will be exercised in mighty ways through the Church in these coming days. This will be part of the spiritual revolution. The Church will walk in the fullness of its authority giving glory to God. Let's get ready and build ourselves up in Him.

## One Final Wave of Glory

Toward the end of our evening's experience with lightning bolts and dragon slaying, the Holy Spirit led us into one more wave of His glory. The glory came in the form of absolute rest of spirit. The weight of His presence rested on us like a heavy blanket. One could have fallen into a deep sleep (which is actually another spiritual experience—see Gen. 2:21). There was an inward sense of satisfaction and we all knew that our "visitation" with Him had concluded for that evening, although He continued to inhabit each one of us. He never leaves us and never withdraws His love, even when we are not having a spiritual visitation. Christ is forever with us even when we are not aware of His manifest presence. How wonderful He is!

Since that evening I have had many more visitations in the realm of the spirit. He has revealed His glory in amazing ways. Sometimes, one experience with God is a door opener to more. That evening was truly that. Along with many on our ministry team, I have enjoyed the glories of the throne room, the heavenly colors, glory clouds, the fire of God, and the winds of the Spirit. The more I seek Him and wait on Him, the more He reveals. He's awesome!

Our time together that night was absolutely remarkable from beginning to end. It was one of those memorable occasions that will never be forgotten. Lightning bolts, Mongolian dragons, and oh, yes, "blessed" coffee and fellowship. What an evening!

# Chapter Ten

# HEAVENLY BEINGS

The appearance of angels and heavenly creatures and beings seems to be earmarking this season of spiritual revolution. Everywhere I travel I find people, both young and old, saved and unsaved, who describe appearances of creatures from the unseen dimension.

In 1995, I received my first open-eye vision of an angelic being. A group of us were engaged in intercession in our home, and as I looked up from prayer, I saw with open vision an enormous heavenly creature. We were gathered in our living room on the first floor, where a two-story open section of our home is overlooked by a dining area on the second-floor balcony. The angel was standing, with its torso filling the entire upper level of the room. The top of its head went through the ceiling. I was able to see one of its wings stretched out over the living room and through the wall to the outside of the house. The span of the wing must have been about 20 feet and its depth about 6 feet. The actual height of the angel could have been well over 20 feet.

I screamed due to the shock I felt as I saw it. No wonder the angels in the Bible regularly encouraged those they visited to "fear not." This angel was an awesome creature, and I was caught off guard. Unfortunately, as soon as I screamed, I lost vision of the angel, which saddened me. Sometimes, our responses in the natural realm jar our sensitivity to the spiritual realm. I did, however, feel a holy presence in our home for about three days following the vision.

I later asked the Lord why He had granted this sovereign angelic visitation. Our ministry had been in a season of very strong assault from a demonic principality at the time, and it seemed as though this angel was ministering assurance to us. Angels are placed on assignment, and one of their functions is *to minister for them who shall be heirs of salvation"* (Heb. 1:14b KJV). Angels' assignments vary as to the need of the believer, but this one definitely gave us a sense of security and protection. Following that time, the warfare seemed to wane, and breakthroughs came. I received further visitations from this angel in the following months and years. I saw it on a ministry tour across Canada where its appearance filled the entire sky in front of me. Also, during a time when I was transported in the spirit to the parliament buildings in our nation, the angel appeared. A man of God whom I highly respect suggested that when the Lord assigns an angel to us, it stays with us for life as "the gifts and callings of God are without repentance." I like the thought of that.

## Angels From the Resource Department in Heaven

A number of years ago, our core team was interceding for a ministry assignment the Lord had given us. To fulfill this assignment, a large amount of finance was required in addition to a level of faith far beyond anywhere we had operated before. During that prayer meeting, I saw a vision of what appeared to be the resource department of Heaven. I saw gold, silver, and commodities of every sort. The Lord declares in Scripture, *"The silver is Mine and the gold is Mine"* (Hag. 2:8a). The Word also assures us that *"God will supply all your needs according to His riches in glory in Christ Jesus"* (Phil. 4:19). Other friends of mine, such as Paul Keith Davis, Charlie Robinson, and Shawn Boltz, have seen similar places in the heavens and have encountered angels who labor in those locations.

During my glimpse into Heaven that day, the Lord showed me that He was going to dispatch angels from the resource department in Heaven to serve our ministry. These angelic ministers help bring the provision that is stored up for God's covenant children and that is needed to fulfill every assignment that God places in our hands. Since that time, we have repeatedly witnessed miraculous provision that has enabled us to fulfill Kingdom assignments, including feeding and clothing the needy of the world as well as meet our own needs and fulfill ministry mandates.

In this era of spiritual revolution, believers will learn how to receive their needs from the unseen and miraculous realm. Too often Christians in the Western world lean to their own understanding and the world's methods when it comes to issues of provision. However, we need to walk in the realm of the supernatural like Jesus did. In the miracle of the loaves and the fishes, Jesus looked toward Heaven and blessed the food (see Mark 6:41). Jesus operated in a heavenly perspective, and He connected with the glory realm. As a result, an awesome miracle was performed. Heaven touched earth! In Second Kings 19:5-8, when Elijah was running from Jezebel, an angel of God came and supplied the prophet with food and drink so that he could be strengthened. This can happen to you too.

The Lord often encourages me to go into the heavenlies and receive provision. I do this by faith as the heavenlies are part of the invisible realm. Following my acts of faith that are led by the Spirit, the provision manifests in the natural realm. At times, I have seen the manifestation come within hours, and other times it happened many months later. There are riches in the presence of the Lord's glory that we can apprehend through our faith, and angels are appointed by God to help us do so.

A number of years ago, I was also visited by an angel of prosperity (one who is given stewardship over resources). It is God's desire that all His children prosper. True Bible prosperity is to enjoy more than enough, and when you are in prosperity, you will always have enough to extravagantly give to the Lord as part of your worship, enough to meet your own needs, and enough left over to help meet the needs of others. The Lord has called us to be blessed so that we can be a blessing. True prosperity has nothing to do with how much money we have in the bank, how much property we own, what brand of clothes we wear, or what type of vehicle we drive. Prosperity is a spiritual force and is not defined by the world's standards.

When the Lord introduced me to the angel of prosperity, He instructed me at times to dispatch this angel in His name to various ministries and individuals. It has been quite remarkable to see the fruitful results as I have followed His leading over the years. He is the God of more than enough, and He has created angels that serve His covenant children in these arenas.

## Angels of All Shapes and Sizes

There are many different types of angels, heavenly beings, and creatures, which have stood in the presence of the Lord for thousands of years. Hence, they carry so much of His glory when they are in our midst. As glorious as they are though, they must not be exalted or worshiped.

They are always around us but seldom are you aware of their presence or their mission. Most of their work is hidden from our attention. Consequently, our focus of worship can remain on Christ. However, during times of increased angelic visitation, believers can receive the gift of discernment in order to recognize their presence and identify them and their assignment.

The early church had numerous visitations from angels. An angel delivered Peter and the other apostles out of prison in Acts 5:18-20 and gave them instructions following their release. In Acts chapter 12, we find Peter in prison again. In verse 7, an angel *"came upon him and a light shined in the prison: and he smote Peter on the side, and raised him up saying, Arise up quickly. And his chains fell from his hands"* (KJV).

When angels are ministering, supernatural and miraculous events can take place. Peter was subsequently led out of prison by the angel and arrived at the home of Mary, the mother of John for a prayer meeting. When Rhoda opened the door, she was shocked and ran to tell the others in the meeting that Peter was there. They couldn't believe it and said to her, *"It is his angel"* (v. 15b KJV).

Perhaps they determined it was his angel because they were accustomed to seeing angels and they were aware that the guardian angel assigned to each individual often looks like that individual. I once saw my angel, and I was amazed at how much its appearance was like mine. It was taller and leaner than I am, but it definitely resembled me. In this time of spiritual revolution, the appearance of angels and heavenly beings will be accelerated. Artists will portray them and music will reveal them.

Recently, I hosted an interview with Akiane, a internationally recognized child prodigy, considered the only known binary genius in both realistic painting and poetry, and she attests to the fact that she received her inspiration through divine visitation at four years of age. She paints heavenly perspectives, Jesus, and angels as she has seen them. Writings and artistic pieces that reflect the visitation of the divine and the angelic in this time of revolution will be recorded in future historical records.

Sometimes during worship, we will hear the angelic choruses joining in our exaltation of Jesus. I have also heard worship recordings where angelic sounds and singing were evident. The musicians involved in these recordings claim that there was no natural means for these sounds.

The first chapter of Hebrews is probably one of the most important portions in the Scripture regarding the awareness of the angelic in their proper perspective. The writer of Hebrews makes it clear that Jesus Christ is the only exalted One and that angels are simply ministering spirits who serve those who are to be heirs of salvation (see Heb. 1:14).

Various types of angels and angelic beings, having different appearances and functions, are recorded in the Bible. Following are descriptions of some of the angelic beings we see in the Scriptures.

### Seraphim

In Isaiah chapter 6, we find the prophet engaged in a "throne zone" experience. In the throne room, we find a particular type of angel called "seraphim." Seraphim means "fiery ones." It is my belief that these angelic beings minister holiness and the purging that comes from fire. It is possible that these beings are even made up of fire. The ministry of these angels purged Isaiah's iniquity and prepared him for his next assignment. Sometimes in our Glory Schools we have the manifestation of the fire of God; you can even tangibly smell the fire at times. Many attest to feeling the heat of the fire touch parts of their bodies just as Isaiah did. Perhaps this manifestation is the visitation of the seraphim.

### Cherubim

God gave Isaiah a vision of seraphim while, for Ezekiel, He gave a vision of the cherubim. The cherubim guarded the tree of life in Genesis 3:24. Later, God instructed Moses to place golden cherubim over the mercy seat (see Ex. 25).

The Book of Ezekiel describes the unusual and awesome appearance of the cherubim and makes it clear that they are stewards of the glory. Cherubim ushered the glory into the temple and removed it when Israel was unrepentant (see Ezek. 10). When the glory of the Lord manifests in meetings, you can often sense the presence of angels as well. During spiritual revolution, the cherubim will be involved with ushering in the glory of the Lord. Let us keep our hearts fervent for the Lord so that these same angelic beings will not be required to remove the glory and cry *"Ichabod"* ("the glory has departed"—see 1 Sam. 4:21).

### Zoa (Living Creatures)

In Revelation 4:6, we find reference to the living creatures around the throne. They are full of eyes in front and behind (as also are the wheels of the cherubim). This is interesting to note, as eyes are the organ that allows us to "see." These creatures carry a powerful revelation of Jesus as they see various dimensions of His nature and character. They cry "Holy, holy, holy" day and night. In a throne room visitation, it is possible to see these creatures as John did. These heavenly beings have the form of eagles, oxen, lions, and humans. I have seen angelic creatures that have eagle forms and have also seen the lions.

## Chariots and Chariot Drivers

In Second Kings 2:12, Elisha saw the heavenly chariot and the horsemen appear when his master Elijah was taken up into glory. The heavenly realm is full of innumerable surprises for us. Have you ever imagined what it would be like to ride in a chariot pulled by angels?

While in a revival meeting on Vancouver Island a number of years ago, I strongly discerned the presence of angels. While I continued to ponder this, the evangelist began to declare, "There is a lot of angelic activity here tonight." It is always encouraging to receive confirmation of a discernment. Those in the crowd who were discerning angels were then invited to come forward, and a number of us responded. The evangelist asked the Lord to release the angels to perform whatever they were called to do. *"For He will give His angels charge concerning you, to guard you in all your ways"* (Ps. 91:11).

Immediately, I found myself sitting in a chariot. I had gone into a trance-type of vision, but what was amazing was that I could actually feel the seat of the chariot under me. I then became aware of darkness all around, and I found myself suddenly being pulled by a team of angels, who were about to take me for the ride of my life!

I heard them laughing uproariously as they whipped me around corners and drew me up, down, and around at breakneck speed, on what seemed like a roller-coaster track, although I did not see anything that resembled that. I gripped tightly on to the side of the chariot while literally feeling a wind blowing across my face. Even though the ride was extremely thrilling, I was still overwhelmed because I couldn't see where we were going. In spite of my uneasiness, the angels certainly appeared to enjoy themselves.

I believe that I was in the vision for approximately ten minutes. When I came out of the vision, I asked the Lord what the purpose of this little excursion was. His answer was simple: "I just wanted you to have fun." Really? You mean, God is into fun? God actually delights in being playful with His children. Perhaps we get too intense and serious at times. Our heavenly Father is to be reverenced at all times, and there are very sober and fearsome sides to Him. Consider Isaiah, while in the revelation of His high and holy presence, declared, *"Woe is me, for I am undone"* (Isa. 6:5) This is one side of God, and we must never lose sight of that. However, He is also playful, loving, and gentle. He is a Father who adores His children. The Lord often has special little surprises along the way that minister refreshment to us. The experience of the chariot ride confirmed to me the reality and tangibility of the unseen realm as well as the Father's tender love and joy. The Word confirms that angelic chariots, chariot drivers, and even spirit horses are for real—they truly are! (See Second Kings 2:11-12; 6:13-17; Zechariah 1:8-11; Psalm 68:17.)

*Chief Princes*

Angels not only have different functions, forms, and shapes, but they vary in rank and position as well. Lucifer, for example, was a high-ranking angel in Heaven before he fell.

Chief princes or archangels are given jurisdiction over land and special events. Michael is referred to in the Scriptures as an archangel or chief prince (see Jude 1:9 and Dan. 10:13). It is believed that Michael oversees warfare and is the chief prince over the affairs of Israel.

Not long ago, at a national prayer assembly in Canada, a prophet received a vision that seems to confirm this role of Michael. Following three days of identificational repentance, this respected prophet saw a vision of the archangel Michael leading an entourage of angels from Israel to Canada. At the time, we had been humbling ourselves before God in repentance for our sinful choices as a nation toward Israel. An historical work of reconciliation took place at that meeting.

Like Michael, the angel Gabriel is also believed to be an archangel. Many prophetic people sense that this high-ranking angel is in charge of communication and special messages. In Scripture, Gabriel was involved when momentous messages were to be heralded. In recent years, I have heard many testimonies from believers who have been visited by angels bringing them messages from the throne room.

### Common Angels

The Scriptures also clearly teach that angels encamp around the righteous—we are surrounded! We have come to an *"innumerable company of angels,"* the writer of Hebrews declares in Hebrews 12:22 (KJV). These angels often minister the purposes and nature of the Lord to us. For example, spirits of wisdom minister the wisdom of the Lord to us. Spirits of revelation minister the revelation of Christ, while spirits of grace minister His grace and favor. God gives each angel a different assignment.

# Increased Awareness of the Angelic

Today, the Body of Christ is becoming increasingly aware of angelic activity. This is a good sign. All throughout the Scriptures, we see evidence of angels and their interaction with man. Whether you sense them or not, angels are all around you—the Word says so! They are wonderful creatures sent to minister the love, grace, and glory of the Lord and His Kingdom.

Following are some Scriptures to study on the subject of angels.

### General Facts About Angels

1. They were created before the earth. Job 38:4-7; Psalm 148:2-5.

2. They are not to be worshiped. Colossians 1:16; Revelation 19:10.

3. They are innumerable. Luke 2:13; Hebrews 12:22.

4. They are subject to God. Matthew 22:30.

### The Works of Angels

1. Bring answers to prayer. Daniel 9:21-28.

2. Minister to the saints. Hebrews 1:14.

3. Worship God. Revelation 5:11; Psalm 148:2.

4. Carry our God's orders. Psalm 103:20.

5. Wage warfare. Revelation 12:7-9; Daniel 10:12-13.

6. Watch over children. Matthew 18:10.

7. Strengthen people during trials. Matthew 4:11.

8. Lead sinners to Gospel workers. Acts 10:3.

9. Direct preachers. Acts 8:26.

10. Appear in dreams. Matthew 1:20-24.

11. Minister before God. Revelation 8:2; 14:15-19.

12. Protect believers from harm. Psalm 91:11; Acts 12:7-10.

13. Guard the Abyss. Revelation 9:1; 20:1-3.

14. Watch over the interest of churches. Revelation 2 and 3.

15. Affects the affairs of nations. Daniel 10:12-13.

16. Extraordinary acts. Acts 7:53; 12:6-7; Galatians 3:9; Hebrews 2:22.

17. Bring God's people special messages. Luke 1.

18. Punish God's enemies. Acts 12:23; 2 Samuel 24:16.

## The Nature of Angels

1. Intelligent and wise. 2 Samuel 14:20; 19:27; Matthew 24:35.

2. Patient. Numbers 11:22-35.

3. Meek. 2 Peter 2:11.

4. Joyful. Luke 15:1-10.

5. Modest. 1 Corinthians 11:10.

6. Holy. Mark 8:38.

7. Glorious. Luke 9:26.

8. Immortal. Luke 20:36.

9. Mighty, powerful. 2 Thessalonians 1:7-10; Revelation 18:1.

10. Obedient. Psalm 103:20; Matthew 6:10.

11. They have wills. Isaiah 14:12-14.

12. Are referred to in most cases as "male." Judges 13:6; Daniel 10:5-21. One reference of "female." Zechariah 5:5-9.

13. Spirit bodies with limbs, eyes, voice, etc. Hebrews 13:2; Judges 13:6; Revelation 15:1-6.

14. They need no rest. Revelation 4:8.

15. They eat food. Genesis 18:8; 19:3; Psalm 78:25.

16. Can appear visible and invisible. Numbers 22:35; John 20:12; Hebrews 13:2.

17. Can operate in the physical realm. Genesis 18:1-19,24; 2 Kings 19:35.

18. They can travel at inconceivable speed. Revelation 8:13; 9:1.

19. They can ascend and descend. Genesis 28:12; John 1:51.

20. They can speak languages. 1 Corinthians 13:1.

## Man's Interaction With Angels

1. Eating angels' food. Psalm 78:25.

2. Led Abraham's servant. Genesis 16:7,9.

3. Moses and the burning bush. Exodus 3:2.

4. Gideon. Judges 6:11-20.

5. Elijah was fed and strengthened. 1 Kings 19:5-8.

6. David (census). 1 Chronicles 21:9-27.

7. Zechariah. Zechariah 1:11-14.

8. Philip. Acts 8:28.

9. Cornelius. Acts 10:3-22.

10. Peter. Acts 12:7-11; Acts 12:15.

11. Herod. Acts 12:23.

12. Paul. Acts 27:23.

13. John. Revelation 2–3.

# Chapter Eleven

# COMMISSIONED
# FOR REVOLUTION

During the spiritual revolution, we will see the restoration of the commission Jesus gave to His Church. Matthew 28:18-20 states: *"All authority has been given to Me in heaven and on earth. Go therefore and make disciples of all the nations, baptizing them in the name of the Father and the Son and the Holy Spirit, teaching them to observe all that I commanded you; and lo, I am with you always, even to the end of the age."*

What were the things Jesus had commanded them that He was now commissioning them to teach to all the nations? In John 14:12, He emphatically declared to His disciples, *"Truly, truly, I say to you, he who believes in Me, the works that I do, he will do also; and greater works than these he will do; because I go to the Father."* Jesus did many amazing works but now He was decreeing that individuals who believe in Him would do the same works and even greater.

Oh how wonderful it would be if we did even a few of the works of Jesus. But if we are honest with ourselves regarding the current state of the Western church, we will have to admit that we are far from the model of Christ. Jesus performed mighty signs and wonders and operated in the supernatural. He encountered angels and the great cloud of witnesses, walked on water, traveled through walls, multiplied food, turned water to wine, healed the sick, raised the dead, cleansed the lepers, and cast out devils. This is the Kingdom of Heaven in action.

Whatever is real in Heaven should be real to us in the earth as we walk in the Kingdom realm. Jesus taught us to pray, "Your Kingdom come, Your will be done on earth as it is in heaven." When we pray those words, do we actually believe them, or has the church been given over to lip service while our heart is far from Him?

As we embrace the spiritual revolution, we will be called to a restoration of Kingdom life, just like Jesus walked in. There is no sickness in Heaven; therefore, we should expect that it will not manifest in our midst, just as it didn't in the life of Jesus. Whenever sick folks asked Jesus for healing, He healed them. He walked in the reality of the Kingdom, and so can we. Jesus also came to destroy the works of the enemy; we have been commissioned to destroy those works as well. Are there demons in Heaven? Of course not. They were given the boot long ago, and yet we tolerate demonic assault in our lives. The revolutionaries who are being raised up in this hour know their authority in Christ and are committed to living it out by faith. Like Paul, they demonstrate the power; they don't just talk about it or preach about it. I want to be such a person.

In Matthew 10:1, Jesus brought His disciples together and gave them authority to cast out demonic spirits and heal every type of sickness and disease. In verses 7 and 8, He sent them off to preach the Kingdom of Heaven and commissioned them to heal the sick, raise the dead, cleanse the lepers, and cast out demons. This is what "preaching the gospel" is to look like. They were to do the same works Jesus did—and they did! So can you, so can I. He said so.

I love the faith of many I have seen in the younger generation. They are radical and going for it! A great example is Todd Bentley who has often challenged my faith. He reads the Word and does the Word. One day he called and said, "Patricia, I bought myself a ticket to Africa. I'm going to cleanse the lepers there." Thinking that this was quite a radical and impulsive decision, I asked him why he thought he needed to go to Africa to cleanse lepers. He replied, "The Bible says that cleansing lepers is part of our Gospel commission. If I don't cleanse the lepers, then I'm not obedient to the Gospel. I looked in Canada for some lepers and couldn't find any so I am going to Africa where I know there is a leper colony." Oh, how I love that faith and obedience. Now, there is a revolutionary!

Heidi Baker, a missionary in Mozambique, also impresses me with her faith. She shared a story with me of how she walked into a hospital where all the babies were sick and dying, having been infected with cholera during an epidemic. She held them in her arms in the midst of vomit and other diseased body excrements and loved them to health without ever contracting a disease, bacteria, or a virus. Her team often holds babies who have died in their arms and loves them to life. That's right, they raise the dead on a regular basis. This is normal Christianity.

Sitting in a church meeting for an hour or so a week, singing some songs, listening to a sermon, and giving some money in the collection plate is not real Christianity. This is not the fullness of the Kingdom. I don't want to suggest that those things are wrong in themselves, but true Kingdom life is much more than that. The spiritual revolution is challenging the way we do church. It is challenging the way we do life!

The following are a few reasons why the Western church is not moving in their God-commanded mandate.

1. **Ignorance.** They have not received teaching and therefore do not understand how to apply their faith to work the works of Jesus and flow in supernatural abilities.

2. **Poor models.** Where are the models of Kingdom life and spirituality in the Western church? Where are those who model the power of God as it is demonstrated in the Bible?

3. **Fear of the supernatural.** Most people fear things they don't understand. Because the Western church has been mainly academic in its orientation, there is uncomfortableness regarding the things that our mind cannot initially understand. Spiritual things need to be spiritually discerned.

4. **Wrong Indoctrination.** Some have received teaching that is contrary to the truth. For instance, in the Pentecostal outpouring in the Azusa Street revival, many reacted against the revival by stating that tongues is of the devil and that believers were to have no part of this. In our day, many contrary doctrines to the Word of God are taught to believers. Things like: prophecy is not for today; women cannot be ordained into ministry; believers cannot have supernatural or heavenly experiences; and only special people can minister healing or preach the Word.

5. **Lack of results.** Some have initially stepped out in faith to perform the works of Jesus, but because they

haven't seen results, they retreat to their comfort zones and neglect to press in.

6. **Unworthiness.** Many believers feel unworthy and as a result do not launch out.

7. **Worldly-mindedness.** The Western church is full of individuals who do not take their spirituality seriously. They attend church sometimes because it is the social thing to do, and they would rather go to a movie than spend time with the Lord.

8. **Prayerlesseness.** Many in the Western church are a prayerless people. The disciples obeyed Jesus and tarried in the upper room until the power came. That happened to be ten full days of continuous and united prayer. Most of us do not spend that amount of time seeking God. In fact, many do not even seek Him more than a few minutes each day. A prayerless church is a powerless church.

9. **Failing to do the Word.** The Scripture says that if we only hear the Word and do not respond by doing it, then our faith is dead. The result—no fruit for our labor because there is no labor.

10. **Sin.** Disobedience to the will of God will always brass over the heavens. Sin is running rampant in much of the Western church, and as a result, we are a powerless church.

11. **Unbelief.** Many will read the Bible and see the record of God's miracles, signs, and wonders but do not believe that it can happen today. Entire denominations have little or no faith in the supernatural operations of the Spirit. Where there is no faith, there is no entrance into the promised land. The Western church is plagued with unbelief.

12. **Associations.** If you hang out with those who are worldly or religiously minded and void of the Spirit, it could possibly rub off on you. You become like the company you keep. In Second Timothy 3:5, the Scripture makes a very strong statement and teaches us to actually avoid individuals who hold to a form of godliness but deny the power. That is a heavy word. I was speaking with a minister recently who explained that a visiting speaker at a conference his ministry was hosting suggested in his public sermon that people should leave a dead church that deny the power. Now, that type of word isn't always very nice. As a result, the ministerial became very upset. I can understand them being upset. If you are a dead church, then you have a right to be upset. On the other hand, if you are flowing in the power and the supernatural, then of course such a statement wouldn't be upsetting at all. In fact, many more people would probably start attending as a result. I am not saying that the minister should have said what he did or not. Only God knows that. What I am saying, though, is that the Word does say to watch associations. Concerning those who deny the power of God, the Word says to "avoid such men as these."

## Where Do We Go From Here?

It is one thing to understand some reasons why we are a powerless church, but how can we actually get the power we need to live a real, supernatural Kingdom life. How can this type of life become normal to us? The following are some suggestions to help cultivate this true heavenly life in you.

1. **Find some good teaching.** There are many valuable seminars, conferences, books, and other resources available to the Body of Christ. Jesus said that you will know a good tree by its fruit. You need to check out various ministries to make sure that the fruit of the Spirit is operating in their lives and ministries and that they have a reputation for teaching the true and inspired Word of God. Our Website at www.extremeprophetic.com has been created for this purpose. We feature many credible Christian prophets and ministers and offer a media site that is full of teaching on the supernatural, prophetic, signs, wonders, healing, deliverance, and prayer. Reading biographies of those who work miracles and operate in the supernatural Kingdom realm is also very helpful.

2. **Put the Word into practice.** If you go to a prophetic seminar, then prophesy. I remember when I was taught to prophesy. After the seminar, I put the gift into practice big time! Before every prayer meeting, church gathering, and Bible study, I would pray and believe for the Lord to give me a word to encourage the people. At the meetings, I would step out in faith, most times with a bit of apprehension, but I went for it. The first year my words were very simple, but they became more specific and profound the more I *practiced.* The same thing happened when I believed the Lord for healing anointing and when I began to step into Third-Heaven experience. You must "do" the word that you believe.

3. **Associate with those who are walking in Kingdom power.** Build friendships with those who have like passion and spiritual hunger. Sometimes, the Lord calls individuals to remain in a stale church environment in order to intercede, love, and bring influence to others in wisdom. If

this is the case, then you must obey the leading of the Spirit. This is your mission field. I personally admire believers who obey the Spirit in these ways. Some, however, might need to plug in to another fellowship where they can grow. In other cases, the Lord might give an opportunity to get involved with an additional ministry that is sound and God-honoring while continuing to attend the local church fellowship. This could fill a void and help growth in the supernatural. We have known many believers who faithfully attend churches not open to the supernatural while at the same time building relationship with our ministry team. This has been very helpful to them as they stay strongly committed to their call to their local assembly. Some Christians live in very remote and isolated areas and have no access to a Spirit-filled church that believes in the supernatural. This is a difficult situation, but with the web media today, good input can come from credible Websites and e-mail articles. Some of our ministry partners live in isolated regions, but they often tell us how connected they feel to us as we build relationship through e-mail, prayer lines, letters, and the Website.

4. **Look for an outlet to minister the Gospel.** Signs, wonders, and supernatural occurrences will follow the proclamation of the Word. God wants us to take His light into the darkness. Look for ways that you can reach the lost.

5. **Fasting and prayer.** As I have studied the lives of revivalists, healing ministers, and those who regularly operate in the supernatural dimension, I have noticed that most of them are given to extended periods of fasting and prayer. Jesus Himself, following a 40-day fast, worked many miracles in the power of the Spirit.

6. **Invite the Holy Spirit to convict you of unconfessed sin that is blocking the pure flow of His power.** It is important to note, however, that God's supernatural power is released and walked in by faith even when there is sin. I have known some ministers who moved in great power and supernatural acts, yet they had secret sin in their lives. The gifts and the callings of God are without repentance, but make no mistake, whatever a man sows he will also reap. Eventually the things done in secret will be exposed and perhaps even shouted from the rooftops! If the Holy Spirit convicts you, then respond with repentance and receive forgiveness and cleansing.

7. **Worship and soaking.** Your fruitfulness will come from intimacy. John chapter 15 teaches us to abide in the Lord. This is the greatest key to Kingdom life. Whatever you focus on, you will empower, so take time to focus each day on Jesus. He is so lovely. Soak in His presence and allow His power to fill and transform you.

8. **Aggressively choose to live in the supernatural.** Oftentimes, we are very passive in our walk with the Lord. We might believe something to be true, yet we don't pursue it. We think, *Oh, maybe God might show up one day and zap me.* Although this could possibly happen, He is actually waiting for us to choose Kingdom life and walk in it. Throughout the Gospels, we see Jesus modeling the supernatural and then inviting His disciples to walk in it. The story of the loaves and fishes in Mark 6:33-44 is a good example. The multitudes with Jesus were hungry, and it was getting late. The disciples suggested that Jesus send them home, but Jesus said, "You give them something to eat." His disciples were shocked at what seemed an impossible task. It wasn't like there were any fast-food

restaurants or grocery stores in the vicinity. Jesus then had them bring to Him what they had (a few loaves and some fish), prayed, and then gave them the pieces to distribute, so that the disciples themselves would work the miracle. They were not supposed to be mere onlookers but active participators in the miraculous works of God. Look for opportunities to move in the supernatural.

## What Is the Spiritual Revolution Going to Look Like?

We have covered a great deal of ground throughout these pages. Each chapter is actually an entire subject in itself that could fill volumes of teaching, establishing foundations and faith in those areas. This book is but a taste of an appetizer that makes us hungry for the main course, and a challenge to walk in the fullness of what the Lord desires for His glorious Church.

What will this glorious Church look like in the midst of spiritual revolution? Perhaps it will look just like Jesus. Maybe we will see the Church emptying hospitals, mental asylums, and even graveyards. Signs, wonders, and miracles will be normal in the time of revolution. Believers will walk through walls, turn water into wine, and feed multitudes with a few loaves and fishes. They will encounter angels and heavenly creatures, ascend and descend into the throne room, soar like eagles in the realm of the spirit, and even move mountains and other objects through supernatural means. The Church will exercise keen prophetic sensitivity and will carry such throne room authority and decree that all who hear will bow their knee to Christ. They will establish moral reform in the earth. The Church in spiritual revolution will know how to live out of a Third-Heaven perspective, refusing to be ensnared by worldly values and ways. God's people in the midst of the coming spiritual revolution will be practicing the things that we read about in the Bible. Kings and entire nations will come to the brightness of the rising of such a people. Hmm...sounds just like the revelation Isaiah had.

> *Arise, shine; for your light has come, and the glory of the Lord has risen upon you. For behold, darkness will cover the earth and deep darkness the peoples; but the Lord will rise upon you and His glory will appear upon you. Nations will come to your light, and kings to the brightness of your rising* (Isaiah 60:1-3).

## Revolutionaries arise, for the spiritual revolution has begun!

## The Glory School

Do you long for deeper experiences with God? Would you like to press in for a more intimate relationship with Him? Well, He is longing for the same with you! The Glory School will help you answer His invitation for more Kingdom experience and divine intimacy! This extensive course is available via live seminar (for a full schedule of upcoming schools go to extremeprophetic.com), or a 16-CD set and manual. In the Glory School you will come to deeply understand the message of the cross, discover how to walk more closely with the Holy Spirit, experience the supernatural presence of God, and much more.

# School of Extreme Prophetic

The Lord is calling! The School of Extreme Prophetic will help you answer. This course is available via live seminar (for a full schedule of upcoming schools go to extreme-prophetic.com), or a 7-CD set and manual. In the School of Extreme Prophetic, you will learn to increase your ability to hear God's voice and share His words of hope and destiny. You will get equipped to go forth, and anointed to reach out to your friends, neighbors and others in creative ways. We live in extreme times, and extreme times call for extreme prophetic!

## Decree

The Word of God is powerful, and it will profoundly influence your life. It does not return void, but accomplishes everything that it is sent to do. Patricia King wrote this booklet to help believers easily activate the power of the word in key areas of their lives including health, provision, love, victory, wisdom, family, business, spiritual strength and many others. The CD contains word decrees spoken over you by Patricia, along with decrees sung over you by Heather Clark.

## Crushing Religious Strongholds and Other Mindsets!

A religious spirit attempts to imprison believers in mindsets that hold to a form of godliness but denies the power of the gospel. Religious spirits are crushed when believers walk in raw Kingdom power. In this 4-CD teaching Patricia King shares about walking in righteousness, embracing heavenly realities, doing "these works and greater," releasing revival, and being a divinely supernatural church that is able to answer the spiritual hunger in the world! These messages will stir you to step out in all Jesus has made available to us!

## The Power Twins – Favor and Honor

Your life can overflow with blessings and benefits! The Power Twins is a two-CD teaching from Patricia King that will help you experience the blessings and benefits of increased favor and honor in your life. Learn to walk in a place of grace and esteem with God and man, and come into the fullness of your destiny.